CLARENDON MEDIEVAL AND TUDOR SERIES

General Editor
J. A. W. BENNETT

CLARENDON MEDIEVAL AND TUDOR SERIES

Already Published

PASTON LETTERS. Selected and Edited with an Introduction, Notes, and Glossary by NORMAN DAVIS. Critical Comment by Horace Walpole, Virginia Woolf, and others. 1958

WILLIAM DUNBAR POEMS. Selected and Edited with an Introduction, Notes, and Glossary by JAMES KINSLEY. Appreciations by John Pinkerton, John Merry Ross, Agnes Mure Mackenzie, W. L. Renwick, C. S. Lewis. 1958

A SELECTION OF ENGLISH CAROLS. Edited with an Introduction, Notes, and Glossary by R. L. GREENE. 1962

SELECTIONS FROM LAЗAMON'S *BRUT*. Edited by G. L. BROOK. With an Introduction by C. S. LEWIS. 1963

ROBERT HENRYSON POEMS. Selected and edited with an Introduction, Notes, and Glossary by CHARLES ELLIOTT. Appreciations by Sir Francis Kinaston, G. Gregory Smith, Edwin Muir and others. 1963

SELECTIONS FROM GAVIN DOUGLAS. With an Introduction, Notes, and Glossary by DAVID F. C. COLDWELL. Appreciations by Thomas Warton, George Saintsbury, C. S. Lewis, E. M. W. Tillyard. 1964

HENRY HOWARD, Earl of Surrey. POEMS. With an Introduction, Notes, and Glossary by EMRYS JONES. Appreciation by Thomas Warton, G. F. Nott, C. S. Lewis, Maurice Evans. 1964

JAMES IV, KING OF SCOTS

WILLIAM DUNBAR
Poems

Appreciations by

JOHN PINKERTON · JOHN MERRY ROSS
AGNES MURE MACKENZIE
W. L. RENWICK · C. S. LEWIS

With an Introduction, Notes
and Glossary by

JAMES KINSLEY

OXFORD
AT THE CLARENDON PRESS

Oxford University Press, Ely House, London W. 1

GLASGOW NEW YORK TORONTO MELBOURNE WELLINGTON
CAPE TOWN SALISBURY IBADAN NAIROBI LUSAKA ADDIS ABABA
BOMBAY CALCUTTA MADRAS KARACHI LAHORE DACCA
KUALA LUMPUR HONG KONG

FIRST PUBLISHED 1958
REPRINTED LITHOGRAPHICALLY AT THE UNIVERSITY PRESS, OXFORD
FROM CORRECTED SHEETS OF THE FIRST EDITION
1964, 1966

PRINTED IN GREAT BRITAIN

PREFACE

THE frontispiece portrait of James IV is reproduced by kind permission of the owner, Col. Stirling of Keir, Dunblane. It was originally in the collection of Charles I at Whitehall, 'done after an ancient water coloured piece'—probably a miniature—by the king's portrait painter Daniel Mytens (1590–1642).

The editor acknowledges with gratitude the help and criticism generously given by Dr. J. A. W. Bennett; the late Sir William Craigie, Mr. David Murison, and Mr. A. J. Aitken, editors of the Scottish Dictionaries; his wife, Mrs. Helen Kinsley; and Mr. H. R. H. Woolford, Keeper of the National Gallery of Scotland. Copyright material is reprinted by kind permission of Miss Jean Mackenzie and Messrs. A. and C. Black, Professor W. L. Renwick and the Cresset Press, and Professor C. S. Lewis and the Clarendon Press.

University College of Swansea
November 1957

CONTENTS

CONTENTS

CONTENTS

* These poems are not printed in full. Omissions are indicated in the text by . . .

(ix)

INTRODUCTION

DUNBAR was a court makar. His poetic inheritance was the courtly tradition of medieval France and England; his professional concern was with the personalities and humours of the court of James IV, King of Scots. The study of his poetry is the study of an aristocratic culture that flowered in a brief time of prosperity and perished with the Scottish chivalry at Flodden, 'whence no great man of Scotland returned home'.

Of Dunbar's royal patron the fullest account is given by Pedro de Ayala, Ferdinand of Spain's ambassador in Scotland, in a dispatch of 25 July 1498. Ayala, who had every reason to be cautious in his judgements, portrays James as the ideal prince: energetic and practical, diplomatic and humane, holding the peace and increasing the prosperity of his country; 'courageous, even more than a king should be', and displaying an impulsive chivalry in battle, 'himself first in danger'; a Stewart with the amorous disposition and the fatal pride of his house—'he esteems himself as much as though he were lord of the world'. Ayala remarks on his command of languages—Latin, French, German, Flemish, Italian, and Spanish, besides his native Scots and Gaelic— and on his knowledge of religious literature and of French and Latin chronicles.[1] We know from other sources of his interest in the fine arts and music, in the new craft of printing, and in alchemy; and the historian Pitscottie says 'he was well learned in the art of medicine, and was a singular good chirurgeane'. There is evidence of his concern for practical education in the endowment of the first British chair of medicine—at Aberdeen in 1495—and the grant of

[1] The Accounts of the Lord High Treasurer of Scotland (1500–4) record purchases of (*inter alia*) biblical commentaries, sermons, devotional and theological works; the Decretals; a Latin translation of Strabo; and editions of Quintilian and Virgil.

a charter to the College of Surgeons in 1506; even more significantly, in the act of 1496 that required all barons and men of property to set their sons to school to be 'competently founded and have perfect Latin, and thereafter to remain three years at the schools of art and jure that they may have knowledge and understanding of the laws, through the which justice may reign universally'. That, however, was basic training for citizenship: courtly education was elaborately humane. In 1507 Erasmus became tutor to the young prince Alexander, archbishop of St. Andrews and 'Marcellus of the Scottish Church', who died with his father at Flodden. His severer studies, says Erasmus, were Greek, rhetoric, and law—'a subject not very pleasing, because of . . . the insufferable verbosity of its expounders'; but

he gave his afternoons to music, to the monochord, flute, or lute; and he sometimes sang while playing on a stringed instrument. Even at mealtime he was not forgetful of his studies. The chaplain always read some good book, such as the Pontifical Decrees, St. Jerome, or St. Ambrose. . . . On the other hand, he liked tales, when they were brief, and when they treated of literary matters. Hence no portion of his life was spent without study, except the hours given to religion and to sleep. If he had any spare time . . . he spent it in reading history, for in that he took extreme delight.[1]

Relics of the architecture and art of the time, the inventories and accounts of the court and colleges, and records of progresses and celebrations, all bespeak a rich material culture, a respect for the new learning, and a court gay with music and splendid with pageantry. But the enduring memorial of James's reign is the poetry of Dunbar. That poetry, moreover, marks the shadows beneath the brightness. It exposes the king's inconstancy as a patron of letters, and the viciousness and expensive charlatanism of the court —there are points of likeness between James IV and his

[1] *Adagia*; in G. Gregory Smith, *The Days of James IV*, 1890, pp. 74-75.

descendant Charles II; and it reflects the 'strange aura' in a contemporary portrait of the King, 'under all the gaiety and the eager brilliance . . . an endurance of dark knowledge'.[1]

Medieval Scottish poetry, like that of England, owes much to France. Diplomatic and cultural links between the two countries were strong, and remained so until the end of the sixteenth century. There were many 'monsouris of France' about the court of James IV. Ayala found 'a good deal of French education in Scotland; and many speak the French language. All the young gentlemen who have no property go to France, and are well received there; and therefore the French are liked.' Dunbar, then, cannot have escaped contact with some of the courtly literature, particularly the lyric poetry, of France. This is not to suggest that his work, in many ways so remote from Chaucer's and so fundamentally French in form and technique, derives directly from French models. His only acknowledged masters are 'reverend Chaucere, rose of rethoris all', 'morall Gower, and Ludgate laureate', English agents for the import of continental literature. He can hardly be called a disciple even of the greatest of these poets; and his vitality and freshness, as well as his confident handling of themes uncommon in Middle English, suggest a vigorous native tradition in Scots.

Dunbar's main debt to English poetry is in rhetoric and 'most mellifluate' diction, which 'oure rude langage has clere illumynate'. The 'aureate' diction of poems like 'Ryght as the stern of day begouth to schyne' is not, as is sometimes supposed, a dubious Scottish invention. It is the northern counterpart of the fifteenth-century English attempt to distil the 'dulcet speche', in the words of Stephen Hawes,

> Electynge words which are expedyent,
> In Latin or in Englyshe, after the entente,
> Encensyng out the aromatyke fume,
> Our langage rude to exyle and consume.

[1] Agnes Mure Mackenzie, *The Rise of the Stewarts*, 1935, pp. 299–300.

Exercises like 'Hale sterne superne' seem bizarre virtuosity nowadays; but the aureate style is splendidly appropriate to allegorical pageantry or royal occasions. Dunbar creates an artificial world of divine harmony and heraldic colour: red and white, purple and silver, green and gold. He does not restrict himself to conventional ornament, to golden sunshine, silver dews, enamelled meads; nor does he manage his gorgeous effects merely by a generous carelessness with paint. He patterns and contrasts as artfully in colour as in sound: a glimpse of flowers from a window—'quhyt, reid, *broun* and blew'—and framed against them the crystal-eyed Aurora with 'visage paill and grene'; a lion, red 'as is the ruby glance' on a field of gold; maidens with 'tressis clere' and 'pappis quhite' gathered in 'kirtillis grene'; and against a red sky, a sail 'als quhite as blossum upon spray'.

Dunbar, says Sir Herbert Grierson, 'has command of two distinct vocabularies—aureate diction bejewelled with French and Latin for pious and courtly work, and for satire and abuse an arsenal of the broadest, coarsest Scots, hard, concrete words that hit his victims like clods of earth'. The distinction is useful, but much too sharply drawn. It is true that Dunbar throws divots, not gems. But in his 'courtly work' there are glisks of pure hard metal beneath the ornament—'stanneris clere as stern in frosty nycht'; and in the battle of the golden targe he turns back to the old harsh language of Barbour, for 'the schour of arowis rappit on as rayn' and 'thik was the schote of grundyn dartis kene'. The virtue of his 'pious work', moreover, is not aureation, but naked strength and triumphant harmony. He uses—or ignores—the categories of language and style to suit his purpose. His vocabulary ranges from 'anamalit termes celicall' to the colloquial Scots of Edinburgh closes and taverns. He has an ear as sensitive as Chaucer's to the quality and pitch of the spoken word; and he transmits the gossip of countrymen and 'cummeris', the frank chatter of women of fashion, and the salacious whispers overheard in a corner of Holyrood, as easily as he assumes the high courtly style or the impersonal exaltation of a hymn. His resources are boldly used. He draws into service, with scant respect for the restrictive proprieties of the 'kinds', aureate words and 'terms of art' from the professions and crafts, tags from the romances and phrases from the Latin of the Church, gnomic colloquialisms, alliterative phrases from both courtly and popular poetry, and obscenities. *The Tretis of the tua mariit Wemen and the Wedo*, juxtaposing the language of romance and the vernacular of the streets, is a grand linguistic joke. Even in the prolonged abuse of the *Flyting* there is an astonishing variety of language: melodramatic rhetoric, a 'langage rude' of calculated harshness and fine precision in the caricature of Kennedy, and a wildly vituperative climax which is as much a *tour de force* in diction as any passage from the aureate poems.[1]

Dunbar's verse forms and metres range from rhyme-royal and shorter stanzas to the couplet and the alliterative line. His modes include allegory and vision, prayer and hymn, elegy and panegyric, dramatic and reflective lyric, comic narrative and satire. The variety of forms is obvious: less obvious, and more important, is the originality with which he handles them. The visions of the thistle and the rose (5) and the golden targe (11) are orthodox 'minuets of conventions'; but the dream device is given a startling vitality in the vision of the Friar of Tungland (15), the burlesque tournament of the tailor and the soutar (18), and the dance of the Seven Deadly Sins (17)—where the carnival procession of the Sins is blended with the *diablerie* of the mystery plays in a whirling pageant of horror. Dunbar tried his hand at the *chanson d'aventure*, as Henryson did; but his setting is a dark corner, not a sunlit meadow, and the conventional protestations of love give way to comic animality (13). The device of the poetic testament is applied in macaronics, with

[1] There is a discussion of 'Dunbar and the Language of Poetry' by Edwin Morgan in *Essays in Criticism*, ii (1952), 138–58.

B

incidental parody of the burial service, to ridicule a drunken doctor in self-destructive monologue (43). The tournament of 1508, 'L'Emprise du Chevalier Sauvage à la Dame Noire', occasions sly mockery of the conventional praise of white beauty (8). Dunbar lures the king back from retreat among the Franciscans to the luxuries of Edinburgh with a devilish parody of the Office for the Dead (44). He uses the metre and conventions of romance, after the example of Chaucer, to silence a court braggart (36). Meditation on death is given dramatic shape in a poetical *danse macabre* (23), for which Dunbar had a splendid model in the stone carvings at Rosslyn in Midlothian. But the traditional number of *morts* —type-figures of prince and prelate, knight and lady, and many more—is restricted to make room for a procession of dead poets; elegy for Chaucer and the older makars rises into lamentation for Henryson and Sir John the Ross, and Kennedy lying 'in poynt of dede'; and a meditative vision ends in a *cri de cœur*. Dunbar introduces no new poetic 'kind', but he is a vigorously creative traditionalist.

His interest in developing contrasts between conventional form and freshly chosen theme is most fully illustrated in his longest poem, *The Tretis of the tua mariit Wemen and the Wedo* (12). The poem is formally a *débat* on love.[1] Three ladies are discovered in a decorated garden bower, celebrating the festival of Midsummer Eve. The poet, following the convenient habit of many courtly predecessors, creeps up and *en cachette* behind a hedge listens to their conversation. In the midst of the feast, the Wedo assumes the role of president of the court, and sets her companions a *demande d'amour*: 'Bewrie . . . quhat mirth ye fand in maryage'; 'think ye it nocht ane blist band?' The ladies take up the question in turn, answering it from their marital experience. When the Wedo has made her contribution, the discussion is resolved in wine and laughter and the trio 'rake hame to

[1] The following comments are reprinted, with permission, from *Medium Ævum*, xxiii (1954), 32–35.

ther rest'. The poet turns to the reader with a satiric *demande* of his own: which of these three 'wantoun wiffis', ii any, would you take as yours?

On the setting of the debate, and on the participants, Dunbar lavishes all the bright colour, ornament, and 'anamalit' diction of the grand style. The 'gudlie grein garth' is a paradise of delight. The ladies are as splendid as their surroundings. Superficially they are 'fair wlonkes' and 'ryall roisis'; they talk of their lovers (not their husbands) in courtly terms; and the Wedo professes the *amour courtois* virtue of 'pitee' and saves her distracted wooers in traditional style (ll. 170–3, 213–18). But this is only a whimsical, jocular echo of courtly sentiment. The Wedo's 'honour' is an accessible commodity, and her exercise of 'pitee' is indiscriminate and over-generous. Her use of the rules and terms of *amour courtois* is deliberately comic, and when she ends her defence of promiscuity as the exercise of 'mercy' her companions laugh loudly and promise to 'wirk efter hir wordis'. She is sister to the Wife of Bath—in appetite and high spirits, in social station and social pride, in uninhibited self-confession, and in her fondness for fine clothes and jewels 'quhill hely raise my renoune amang the rude peple'. Her companions, in background and in speech, are citizens rather than ladies of the court; Edinburgh 'cummeris', hilariously bawdy over their wine. Dunbar characteristically places them between two extremes. He draws a satirical contrast between their superficial beauty and delicacy, and their essential coarseness and corruption; but even while they expose their real nature, they comically retain the trappings of courtly grace in a familiarity with 'poetic' and *amour courtois* terms. Ideal beauty is revealed as the whited sepulchre of lust, and what seems to be of the bower is seen to belong to the street—and at the same time three drinking gossips cynically pretend, as part of their festive joke, to hold allegiance to courtly love.

In the *Tretis* the alliterative line is used on two levels.

By the time of James IV this metre had come to be associated with sophisticated courtly poetry; and in his prologue Dunbar shows a familiarity with the diction and devices of the 'alliterative revival'. For more than forty lines, the smooth run of the verse and the rich poetic phraseology give the listener what he expects in this measure, and seem to set the tone of the poem. Metre, diction, and the external character of the three women harmonize. Then the alliterative line, losing nothing in flexibility and compactness but gradually increasing in force, is turned to a new and unexpected use in the speech of the first wife. The centre of the *Tretis* is the contrast between appearance and reality, between the ideal world of courtly poetry and the 'spotted actuality' of the three women's minds and habits; and to this end a metrical form associated with high style and sophisticated matter is turned into the medium of coarse erotic reminiscence.

In craftsmanship Dunbar surpasses most medieval poets and all other Scots poets—a passion for form and finish is not conspicuous in Scottish literature. Has he anything more to offer his reader? His eye seldom reached beyond the fringe, or his mind beneath the surface, of that now remote Stewart court which was his milieu. He does not share Chaucer's (or even Henryson's) interest in philosophy and letters. His didactic and reflective verse is smooth without depth, subtle only in style and changing mood: he expresses the melancholy temper of his age with fine simplicity, but there is no provocative questioning, no restless seeking 'after the whyes'. He has little of the compassion of a Chaucer or a Burns.

Yet he has two important qualities besides sheer style— an original humour, and imagination; and in him the two are complementary. He had not Chaucer's facility for making conventional dreams seem real. His 'aureate' visions are not seen and felt; they are constructed in paint, and the artist's preoccupation is with what is on his canvas and not with the visual reality. The seething life of town and court, on the

other hand, he depicts with open-eyed delight—the throng of charlatans and eccentrics about the king, the bustle of market and law-court, whores and gallants and rogues in the street, a fat gossip wheezing by a tavern fire, the revealing capers and gestures of those that danced in the queen's chamber, and the disorderly rabble that 'claschit' Kennedy.

Realistic genre-painting is not, however, his natural mode (and here he stands apart from the main tradition of Scottish poetry). What is most distinctive in his genius is a wild comic fantasy, an extravagance of vision and expression which appears fitfully in some anonymous pieces of grotesquerie from Dunbar's time, but almost passed out of Scots poetry at the Reformation. This extravagance is the essence of the dance of the Seven Deadly Sins, the tale of the Friar of Tungland, the cartoons of Kennedy in the *Flyting*, and the two attributions (45, 46). Dunbar's energy is not only, like Dryden's, an energy of utterance; it is also an energy of imagination.

He has been called, with reason, a 'daft' and 'eldritch' poet, 'possessed of a riotous and fantastic devil'; but his demon is leashed. There is a terrible hammered precision about the pageant of the Sins. The wild, wheeling measure—the dynamism of the devil-dance—is under severe restraint. Written in a similar metre, the blither vision of the Friar shows—for all its extravagance—the same fundamental control. Through all his satiric catalogues, cataracts of abuse, and vertiginous flights of fancy beyond the middle earth, Dunbar never abandons craft to impulse. 'The people of Scotland', says Sir Herbert Grierson, 'have never taken Dunbar to their hearts: "he wants the natural touch".' But he is their finest artist, if not their greatest poet.

BIOGRAPHICAL AND TEXTUAL NOTE

LITTLE is known of Dunbar's life. Born *c.* 1460, he was probably of the 'nobill strynd' of the earls of Dunbar and March. He may have been the William Dunbar who took a bachelor's degree at St. Andrew's in 1477 and a master's degree in 1479. There is no documentary evidence for his activities between 1479 and 1500: that he was a Franciscan novice, and travelled abroad first as a preaching friar and later in the king's service, are speculative deductions from his poems. In 1501 he was in England, probably in connexion with the arrangement of the marriage of James IV and Princess Margaret.[1] He had taken priest's orders by 1504. He was granted a royal pension of £10 in 1500, 'to be pait to him of soverane lordis cofferis be the thesaurair for al the dais of his life or quhil he be promovit be oure soverane lord to a benefice of xl lib. or abone'. By 1507 this had been raised to £20, and he received a 'pensioun most preclair' of £80 in 1510. It is unlikely that he followed the king to Flodden in 1513. He seems to have survived into the new reign, and probably acquired his long-sought benefice since his pension disappears from the accounts after 1513.

There are complete editions of the poems by J. Small and W. Gregor (Scottish Text Society, 3 vols., 1884–9) and by W. Mackay Mackenzie (1932). The fullest account of the biographical evidence is in J. W. Baxter, *William Dunbar* (1952).

This edition contains the greater part of the verse assigned to Dunbar in early manuscript collections, and two poems which in the editor's view may reasonably be attributed to him on internal evidence. Where a poem survives in more than one version, the earliest has generally been preferred unless seriously defective: the text of some poems has been

[1] The poem 'London, thou art the flour of Cities all', which is associated with this visit, cannot be safely ascribed to Dunbar.

constructed from two incomplete versions. The poems are preserved in (1) a number of black-letter prints which survive in apparently unique copies in the National Library of Scotland, and are mainly the work of the Edinburgh printers Walter Chepman and Androw Myllar in or about 1508,[1] and (2) four manuscript collections: the Asloan MS. dating from the early sixteenth century and now in the possession of the Malahide family in Dublin;[2] the Bannatyne MS., compiled by an Edinburgh merchant 'in tyme of pest' in 1568, and now in the National Library of Scotland;[3] the Maitland Folio MS., compiled for Sir Richard Maitland of Lethington between 1570 and 1585, and now in the Pepysian Library, Magdalene College, Cambridge;[4] and the Reidpeth MS. (1622), a transcript of the Maitland MS. which preserves a number of poems now missing from the original, and is now in the University Library at Cambridge.[5]

The Prints and MSS. have been closely followed, but þ and 3 are here printed *th* and *y*, and *u*, *v*, and *w* have generally been given their modern values. Merely scribal devices have been ignored. The punctuation is editorial. Lacunae and emendations are marked by square brackets.

[1] The source of Nos. 7, 11, 12, 23, 43, and 45 in this edition. A facsimile of the Prints, with a note by William Beattie, was published by the Edinburgh Bibliographical Society in 1950.

[2] Scottish Text Society, 2 vols., 1923–5. Nos. 4 and 46 in this edition.

[3] S.T.S., 4 vols., 1928–34. Nos. 1, 3, 5, 10, 14–20, 25, 28, 30, 31, 34, 41, and 44 in this edition.

[4] S.T.S., 2 vols., 1919 and 1927. Nos. 2, 8, 9, 12, 13, 21, 24, 26, 27, 29, 33, 34–40, and 42 in this edition.

[5] Nos. 6, 22, and 32 in this edition.

APPRECIATIONS

THE Historian of English poetry[1] passing to the Scotish poets of this time, says, 'the Scotish writers have adorned the present period with a degree of sentiment, and spirit, a command of phraseology, and a fertility of imagination not to be found in any English poet since Chaucer and Lydgate.' He might safely have added, 'nor even in Chaucer, or Lydgate.' The same excellent judge of poetry observes that the natural complexion of 'Dunbar's genius is of a moral, or didactic cast:' but this remark must not be taken too strictly. The *Goldin Terge* is moral; and so are many of his small pieces: but humour, description, allegory, great poetical genius, and a vast wealth of words, all unite to form the 'complexion' of Dunbar's poetry. He unites in himself, and generally surpasses, the qualities of the chief old English poets; the morals and satire of Langland; Chaucer's humour, poetry, and knowledge of life; the allegory of Gower; the description of Lydgate.

JOHN PINKERTON
Ancient Scotish Poems (1786)

WHEN we consider the originality, strength, and richness of Dunbar's genius, we have no scruple in assigning him the highest place after Burns in the ranks of Scottish poets. Both are distinguished for their force and intensity, their command of terse and graphic language, their daring humour, and their keen insight into the workings of the human heart. Both were galled by poverty and discontented with their lot. Both assailed the favourites of fortune with mingled ridicule and rancour. . . . There is no trace in Dunbar of that glowing humanity which warms the verse of Burns. . . . Love

---

[1] Thomas Warton: see *The History of English Poetry* (1774–81), Sect. xxx.

to him, when it is not allegorical moonshine, is simply lust.
. . . But he has merits almost of the highest kind. His humour
is as deep as that of Burns . . . and more imaginative. *Tam o'
Shanter* is not so marvellous a creation as *The Dance of the
Sevin Deidly Synnis*, though we may find it easier to ap-
preciate the modern poem, in which the tipsy hilarity of the
hero gives a familiar aspect to the devilry of the witches, and
robs it of the weirdness and horror that should mark the
spectacle of a supernatural world. . . .

Dunbar is the first Scot in whose literature we recognise
the distinctive features of the national character, . . . the
first Scottish author who strikes us not only with a sense of
originality, but of dissimilarity from all his predecessors on
both sides of the Tweed. Everything he has written, at least
everything of moment, has a certain unique intensity of
feeling and pith of language that give it a peculiarly national
stamp. This quality of passionate or indomitable force, ever
tending to extravagance and one-sided zeal, distinguishes
and differentiates the people of the North. . . .

Dunbar has this quality of intensity in a remarkable
degree. It gives a richer glow to his landscapes, a grimmer
humour to his satire, a more fearless license to his language,
a deeper gravity to his reflections, and a more nervous vigour
to his verse than other poets of equal or even superior
genius can boast. It has tempted critics of high respectability
to exalt him above Chaucer; and it has led Scott, whose
literary judgment is generally sound, into a panegyric that
requires abatement. . . . Whatever Dunbar attempted, he did
as well as Chaucer, often, indeed, with greater animation
and lavish wealth of words; but if he has the national
vigour, he has also the national narrowness. Chaucer has an
immensely wider vision, and, therefore, immensely broader
sympathies. . . . [Dunbar] rarely gets clear of the atmosphere
of court, of its ambitions, its intrigues, and its scandals. When
he looks abroad upon society it is not with the genial and
sympathetic humour of his great master, but with an in-

tolerant scorn that everywhere finds matter for reprobation or mockery.

JOHN MERRY ROSS
Early Scottish History and Literature (1884)

[DUNBAR] has a fine firm intellectual quality; an intense degree of the 'more than ordinary organic sensibility' that Wordsworth considered the essential of the creative temperament; and a spectacular technical accomplishment. But he comes in an age that all over Europe is almost devoid of spiritual intensity, and his experience rarely brought him the intensity of emotion that, poetically speaking, might have made up for it. He was a priest and a courtier together, one of

> Those gay abati with the well-turn'd leg
> And rose i' the hat-brim, not so much St Paul
> As saints of Caesar's household—

—the type of the eighteenth century *abbé de salon*. Now, priests have written great poems, and so have courtiers, but the combination is a hampering one for the highest kind of poetry. The man who is both can never be wholly either, can never, at heart, desire wholly what is of either, with a sense that the desire, however far from his power, is within his right. Dunbar thus remains below the pinnacles: he writes superb court-poetry, but though he can dance divinely he seldom soars. And partly because of that very limitation it is he of all Northern European poets who most fully expresses the spirit of his own age, its intricate, rather brutal gorgeousness, its hard intellectual quality, its intense vitality of will and the senses and its numbness of the finer spiritual perceptions.

AGNES MURE MACKENZIE
An Historical Survey of Scottish Literature (1933)

IT is pleasant to trace the things Dunbar and Chaucer had in common, and how, even in these, they differed. The difference is almost climatic—between the Thames-side garden and the bleak ridges of Edinburgh and Stirling. Both men disliked the regular orders of clergy: compare *The Somnour's Tale* and *How Dunbar was desierit to be a Frier*. Both were much about courts: compare any of Chaucer's polite, composed court-poems with *The Dance in the Queen's Chalmer*. Both had fits of melancholy: compare the *Envoy to Scogan* with *Timor Mortis Conturbat Me*. Comparison comes to a speedy end. *Troilus and Criseyde* stands clear of all comparisons, then or afterwards ... Dunbar took warning, if he needed it, not to begin anything like *The Legend of Good Women* or *The Monk's Tale* ; he was incapable of anything like the Prologue to the *Legend*, or, for that matter, the Prologue to the *Tales*. On the other hand he could manage a fabliau with anybody; and he was possessed of a riotous and fantastic devil that never haunted Chaucer or the banks of Thames. It is a familiar spirit of the north, lewd, foul, comic both in joy and despair, infinitely vigorous. Skelton knew it, but Skelton's is a ragged double-shuffle compared with the accurately-executed enormities of Dunbar when he set himself capering. It is not satire, nor burlesque, but something on the far and windy side of both. Turn the page, and in *Suete Rois of Vertew*, or *Rorate Coeli Desuper*, the torch-flare changes to cool summer morning or the light of altar-candles. Dunbar's moods are as incalculable as his attitudes: aristocrat, sinner, worshipper at the feet of Our Lady, painter by turns in the school of Hieronymus Bosch and Holbein, he postures, kneels—and disappears. If there are two men to study in all our history from *Beowulf* to Skelton, they are Chaucer and Dunbar.

W. L. RENWICK
The Beginnings of English Literature (1939)

Some of Dunbar's finest work was done in religious poetry of a more ordinary kind. He does not deal much in solitary devotional feeling, like the Metaphysicals or the Victorians; he is public and liturgical. His two supreme achievements in this vein are his poems on the Nativity and on the Resurrection. The first of these (*Rorate celi desuper*) might almost claim to be in one sense the most lyrical of all English poems —that is, the hardest of all English poems simply to *read*, the hardest not to sing. We read it alone and at night—and are almost shocked, on laying the book down, to find that the choir and organ existed only in our imagination. It has none of the modern—the German or Dickensian—attributes of Christmas. It breathes rather the intoxication of universal spring and summons all Nature to salute 'the cleir sone quhome no clud devouris'. . . . I would hesitate to read Milton's Hymn on the same evening with this. The 'Resurrection' is equally, but differently, excellent. It is speech rather than song, but speech of unanswerable and thundering greatness. From the first line ('Done is a battell on the Dragon blak') to the last (*Surrexit Dominus de sepulchro*) it vibrates with exultant energy. It defies the powers of evil and has the ring of a steel gauntlet flung down.

In a poem by Skelton anything may happen, and Skelton has no more notion than you what it will be. That is his charm; the charm of the amateur. But Dunbar is professional through and through; the accomplished master of one tradition that goes back to *Beowulf* and of another that goes back to the Troubadours. All his effects are calculated and nearly all are successful; the last line of each poem was in view before he wrote the first. His harsh and poignant sense of mortality—'Deth followis lyfe with gaipand mowth'— he shares with many late medieval lyrists, notably with Villon, but Villon, so far as I know or remember, lacks his gay splendour. Horace . . . and perhaps Dryden are the poets that seem to me to resemble him most, in the sense that all three are men of strongly masculine genius, professional to the point of virtuosity, and much in love with the languages they write. But, of course, Dunbar is very unlike them in his eldritch quality, and no two sorts of indecency could be more different than his and Dryden's. He is likely to be underrated rather than overrated in our own age. He seems to tell us much about himself—his headache, his lean purse, his pretence that he has other reasons than poverty for not going with his friends to the tavern—but his poems are not 'human documents'. We remain his audience, not his confidants, cut off from him (as it were) by the footlights; and though he can describe real Nature when he chooses, he prefers to transform her, giving his nightingale 'angell fedderis', making his animals heraldic, and turning even lawns and hedges into a kind of jewelry. For both reasons he will in our time be more often admired than loved; a reaction with which he would have been quite content. But he was a very great man. When you are in the mood for it, his poetry has a sweep and volume of sound and an assured virility which (while the mood lasts) makes most other poets seem a little faint and tentative and half-hearted. If you like half-tones and nuances you will not enjoy Dunbar; he will deafen you.

C. S. LEWIS
English Literature in the Sixteenth Century (1954)

DIVINE POEMS

I

RORATE celi desuper.
Hevins distill your balmy schouris,
For now is rissin the bricht day ster
Fro the ros Mary, flour of flouris;
The cleir sone quhome no clud devouris,　　5
Surmunting Phebus in the est,
Is cummin of his hevinly touris
Et nobis Puer natus est.

Archangellis, angellis, and dompnationis,
Tronis, potestatis, and marteiris seir,　　10
And all ye hevinly operationis,
Ster, planeit, firmament, and speir,
Fyre, erd, air, and watter cleir,
To him gife loving, most and lest,
That come in to so meik maneir　　15
Et nobis Puer natus est.

Synnaris, be glaid and pennance do
And thank your makar hairtfully,
For he that ye mycht nocht cum to
To yow is cummin full humly;　　20
Your saulis with his blud to by
And lous yow of the feindis arrest,
And only of his awin mercy
Pro nobis Puer natus est.

All clergy do to him inclyne　　25
And bow unto that barne benyng,
And do your observance devyne
To him that is of kingis king;
Ensence his altar, reid and sing

(1)

In haly kirk, with mynd degest,   30
Him honouring attour all thing
Qui nobis Puer natus est.

Celestiall fowlis in the are,
Sing with your nottis upoun hicht,
In firthis and in forrestis fair   35
Be myrthfull now, at all your mycht;
For passit is your dully nycht,
Aurora hes the cluddis perst,
The son is rissin with glaidsum lycht,
Et nobis Puer natus est.   40

Now spring up, flouris, fra the rute,
Revert yow upwart naturaly,
In honour of the blissit frute
That rais up fro the rose Mary;
Lay out your levis lustely,   45
Fro deid tak lyfe now at the lest
In wirschip of that Prince wirthy
Qui nobis Puer natus est.

Syng hevin imperiall most of hicht,
Regions of air mak armony;   50
All fishe in flud and foull of flicht
Be myrthfull and mak melody;
All *Gloria in excelsis* cry,
Hevin, erd, se, man, bird, and best:
He that is crownit abone the sky   55
Pro nobis Puer natus est.

2

AMANG thir freiris within ane cloister
    I enterit in ane oritorie,
And knelit doun with ane pater noster
    Befoir the michtie king of glorie,

Haveing his passioun in memorie;   5
Syn to his mother I did inclyne,
    Hir halsing with ane *gaude flore*;
And sudandlie I sleipit syne.

Methocht Judas with mony ane Jow
    Tuik blissit Jesu our salvatour,   10
And schot him furth with mony ane schow,
    With schamefull wourdis of dishonour;
    And lyk ane theif or ane tratour
Thay leid that hevinlie prince most hie
    With manassing attour messour,   15
O mankynd, for the luif of the.

Falslie condamnit befoir ane juge,
    Thai spittit in his visage fayr,
And as lyounis with awfull ruge
    In yre thai hurlit him heir and thair,   20
    And gaif him mony buffat sair
That it wes sorrow for to se;
    Of all his claythis thay tirvit him bair,
O mankynd, for the luif of the.

Thay terandis, to revenge thair tein,   25
    For scorne thai cled him in to quhyt,
And hid his blythfull glorious ene,
    To se quham angellis had delyt;
    Dispituouslie syn did him smyt,
Saying, 'Gif sone of God thow be,   30
    Quha straik the now, thow tell us tyt';
O mankynd, for the luf of the.

In tene thai tirvit him agane,
    And till ane pillar thai him band;
Quhill blude birst out at everie vane   35
    Thai scurgit him bayth fut and hand;
    At everie straik ran furth ane strand

(3)   C

Quhilk mycht have ransonit warldis thre;
  He baid in stour quhill he mycht stand,
O mankynd, for the luif of the.   40

Nixt all in purpyr thay him cled,
  And syne with thornis scharp and kene
His saikles blude agane thai sched,
  Persing his heid with pykis grene;
  Unneis with lyf he micht sustene   45
That croune, on thrungin with crueltie,
  Quhill flude of blude blindit his ene,
O mankynd, for the luif of the.

Ane croce that wes bayth large and lang
  To beir thay gaif this blissit lord,   50
Syn fullelie, as theif to hang,
  Thay harlit him furth with raip and corde;
  With blude and sweit was all deflorde
His face, the fude of angellis fre;
  His feit with stanis was revin and scorde, 55
O mankynd, for the luif of the.

Agane thay tirvit him bak and syd
  Als brim as ony baris woid,
The clayth that claif to his cleir syd
  Thai raif away with ruggis rude,   60
  Quhill fersly followit flesche and blude
That it was pietie for to se:
  Na kynd of torment he ganestude,
O mankynd, for the luif of the.

Onto the crose of breid and lenth,   65
  To gar his lymmis langar wax,
Thai straitit him with all thair strenth,
  Quhill to the rude thai gart him rax;
  Syne tyit him on with greit irne takkis,

(4)

And him all nakit on the tre 70
    Thai raissit on loft be houris sax,
O mankynd, for the luif of the.

Quhen he was bendit so on breid
    Quhill all his vanis brist and brak,
To gar his cruell pane exceid 75
    Thai leit him fall doun with ane swak,
Quhill cors and corps all did crak.
Agane thai rasit him on hie,
    Reddie mair turmentis for to mak,
O mankynd, for the luif of the. 80

Betuix tuo theiffis the spreit he gaif
    On to the fader most of mïcht;
The erde did trimmill, the stanis claif,
    The sone obscurit of his licht,
    The day wox dirk as ony nicht, 85
Deid bodiis rais in the cite:
    Goddis deir sone all thus was dicht,
O mankynd, for the luif of the.

In weir that he was yit on lyf
    Thai ran ane rude speir in his syde, 90
And did his precious body ryff
    Quhill blude and water did furth glyde:
    Thus Jesus with his woundis wyde
As martir sufferit for to de
    And tholit to be crucifyid, 95
O mankynd, for the luif of the.

Methocht Compassioun, vode of feiris,
    Than straik at me with mony ane stound,
And for Contritioun, baithit in teiris,
    My visage all in watter drownd; 100
    And Reuth into my eir ay rounde,
'For schame, allace, behald man how
    Beft is with mony ane wound
Thy blissit salvatour Jesu.'

Than rudelie come Remembrance,   105
    Ay rugging me withouttin rest,
Quhilk crose and nalis scharp, scurge and lance
    And bludy crowne befoir me kest;
    Than Pane with passioun me opprest,
And evir did Petie on me pow,   110
    Saying, 'Behald how Jowis hes drest
Thy blissit salvatour Chryst Jesu.'

With greiting glaid be than come Grace
    With wourdis sweit saying to me,
'Ordane for him ane resting place   115
    That is so werie wrocht for the,
    That schort within thir dayis thre
Sall law undir thy lyntell bow,
    And in thy hous sall herbrit be
Thy blissit salvatour Chryst Jesu.'   120

Than swyth Contritioun wes on steir
    And did eftir Confessioun ryn,
And Conscience me accusit heir
    And kest out mony cankerit syn;
    To rys Repentence did begin   125
And out at the yettis did schow.
    Pennance did walk the house within.
Byding our salvatour Chryst Jesu.

Grace become gyd and governour,
    To keip the house in sicker stait   130
Ay reddy till our salvatour,
    Quhill that he come, air or lait;
    Repentence ay with cheikis wait
No pane nor pennence did eschew
    The house within ever to debait,   135
Onlie for luif of sweit Jesu.

For grit terrour of Chrystis deid
    The erde did trymmill quhair I lay,

Quhairthrow I waiknit in that steid
　With spreit halflingis in effray:　　　　140
　Than wrayt I all without delay,
Richt heir as I have schawin to yow,
　Quhat me befell on Gud Fryday
Befoir the crose of sweit Jesu.

3

DONE is a battell on the dragon blak,
Our campioun Chryst confountet hes his force;
The yettis of hell ar brokin with a crak,
The signe triumphall rasit is of the croce,
The divillis trymmillis with hiddous voce,　　　5
The saulis ar borrowit and to the blis can go,
Chryst with his blud our ransonis dois indoce:
Surrexit dominus de sepulchro.

Dungin is the deidly dragon Lucifer,
The crewall serpent with the mortall stang,　　　10
The auld kene tegir with his teith on char
Quhilk in a wait hes lyne for us so lang,
Thinking to grip us in his clowis strang:
The mercifull lord wald nocht that it wer so,
He maid him for to felye of that fang:　　　15
Surrexit dominus de sepulchro.

He for our saik that sufferit to be slane
And lyk a lamb in sacrifice wes dicht,
Is lyk a lyone rissin up agane,
And as a gyane raxit him on hicht:　　　20
Sprungin is Aurora radius and bricht,
On loft is gone the glorius Appollo,
The blisfull day depairtit fro the nycht:
Surrexit dominus de sepulchro.

(7)

The grit victour agane is rissin on hicht   25
That for our querrell to the deth wes woundit;
The sone that wox all paill now schynis bricht,
And, dirknes clerit, our fayth is now refoundit:
The knell of mercy fra the hevin is soundit,
The Cristin ar deliverit of thair wo,   30
The Jowis and thair errour ar confoundit:
Surrexit dominus de sepulchro.

The fo is chasit, the battell is done ceis,
The presone brokin, the jevellouris fleit and flemit,
The weir is gon, confermit is the peis,   35
The fetteris lowsit and the dungeoun temit,
The ransoun maid, the presoneris redemit,
The feild is win, ourcummin is the fo,
Dispulit of the tresur that he yemit:
Surrexit dominus de sepulchro.   40

4

HALE, sterne superne, hale in eterne
    In Godis sicht to schyne:
Lucerne in derne for to discerne
    Be glory and grace devyne:
Hodiern, modern, sempitern,   5
    Angelicall regyne,
Our tern inferne for to dispern,
    Helpe, rialest rosyne.
        Ave Maria, gracia plena,
    Haile, fresche floure femynyne;   10
Yerne us, guberne, virgin matern,
    Of reuth baith rute and ryne . . .

Empryce of prys, imperatrice,
    Brycht polist precious stane,
Victrice of vyce, hie genetrice   15
    Of Jhesu, lord soverayne:

(8)

Our wys pavys fra enemys
　　Agane the feyndis trayne,
Oratrice, mediatrice, salvatrice,
　　To God gret suffragane:　　　　　　　　　20
　　　　Ave Maria, gracia plena,
　　Haile, sterne meridiane,
Spyce, flour delice of paradys
　　That baire the gloryus grayne.

Imperiall wall, place palestrall　　　　　　　25
　　Of peirles pulcritud:
Tryumphale hall, hie trone regall
　　Of Godis celsitud:
Hospitall riall, the lord of all
　　Thy closet did include,　　　　　　　　　30
Bricht ball cristall, ros virginall,
　　Fulfillit of angell fude.
　　　　Ave Maria, gracia plena,
　　Thy birth has with his blude
Fra fall mortall, originall,　　　　　　　　　35
　　Us raunsound on the rude.

5

QUHEN Merche wes with variand windis past,
And Appryll had with hir silver schouris
Tane leif at Nature with ane orient blast,
And lusty May that muddir is of flouris
Had maid the birdis to begyn thair houris   5
Amang the tendir odouris reid and quhyt,
Quhois armony to heir it wes delyt:

In bed at morrow, sleiping as I lay,
Me thocht Aurora with hir cristall ene
In at the window lukit by the day   10
And halsit me, with visage paill and grene;
On quhois hand a lark sang fro the splene,
'Awalk, luvaris, out of your slomering,
Se how the lusty morrow dois up spring.'

Me thocht fresche May befoir my bed upstude   15
In weid depaynt of mony divers hew,
Sobir, benyng, and full of mansuetude,
In brycht atteir of flouris forgit new,
Hevinly of color, quhyt, reid, broun and blew,
Balmit in dew, and gilt with Phebus bemys   20
Quhill all the hous illumynit of hir lemys.

'Slugird', scho said, 'awalk annone for schame,
And in my honour sum thing thow go wryt;
The lork hes done the mirry day proclame
To rais up luvaris with confort and delyt,   25
Yit nocht incresis thy curage to indyt,
Quhois hart sum tyme hes glaid and blisfull bene
Sangis to mak undir the levis grene.'

'Quhairto', quod I, 'sall I uprys at morrow?
For in this May few birdis herd I sing;   30
Thai haif moir caus to weip and plane thair sorrow,
Thy air it is nocht holsum nor benyng:
Lord Eolus dois in thy sessone ring;
So busteous ar the blastis of his horne,
Amang thy bewis to walk I haif forborne.'   35

With that this lady sobirly did smyll,
And said, 'Uprys and do thy observance;
Thow did promyt in Mayis lusty quhyle
For to discryve the Ros of most plesance.
Go se the birdis how thay sing and dance,   40
Illumynit our with orient skyis brycht,
Annamyllit richely with new asur lycht.'

Quhen this wes said, depairtit scho, this quene,
And enterit in a lusty gairding gent;
And than me thocht full hestely besene   45
In serk and mantill [eftir hir] I went
In to this garth, most dulce and redolent
Off herb and flour and tendir plantis sueit
And grene levis doing of dew doun fleit.

The purpour sone with tendir bemys reid   50
In orient bricht as angell did appeir,
Throw goldin skyis putting up his heid;
Quhois gilt tressis schone so wondir cleir
That all the world tuke confort, fer and neir,
To luke upone his fresche and blisfull face   55
Doing all sable fro the hevynnis chace.

And as the blisfull soune of cherarchy
The fowlis song throw confort of the licht:
The birdis did with oppin vocis cry,
'O luvaris fo, away, thow dully nycht,   60
And welcum day that confortis every wight;

(11)

Haill May, haill Flora, haill Aurora schene,
Haill princes Natur, haill Venus luvis quene.'

Dame Natur gaif ane inhibitioun thair
To fers Neptunus and Eolus the bawld,   65
Nocht to perturb the wattir nor the air;
And that no schouris nor blastis cawld
Effray suld flouris nor fowlis on the fold,
Scho bad eik Juno, goddes of the sky,
That scho the hevin suld keip amene and dry.   70

Scho ordand eik that every bird and beist
Befoir hir hienes suld annone compeir,
And every flour of vertew, most and leist,
And every herb be feild fer and neir,
As thay had wont in May fro yeir to yeir   75
To hir thair makar to mak obediens,
Full law inclynnand with all dew reverens.

With that annone scho send the swyft ro
To bring in beistis of all conditioun;
The restles suallow commandit scho also   80
To feche all fowll of small and greit renown;
And to gar flouris compeir of all fassoun
Full craftely conjurit scho the yarrow,
Quhilk did furth swirk als swift as ony arrow.

All present wer in twynkling of ane e,   85
Baith beist and bird and flour, befoir the quene:
And first the Lyone, gretast of degre,
Was callit thair, and he most fair to sene
With a full hardy contenance and kene
Befoir dame Natur come, and did inclyne   90
With visage bawld and curage leonyne.

This awfull beist full terrible wes of cheir,
Persing of luke and stout of countenance,
Rycht strong of corpis, of fassoun fair but feir,
Lusty of schaip, lycht of deliverance,   95

(12)

Reid of his cullour as is the ruby glance:
On feild of gold he stude full mychtely,
With flour delycis sirculit lustely.

This lady liftit up his cluvis cleir
And leit him listly lene upone hir kne,   100
And crownit him with dyademe full deir
Off radyous stonis, most ryall for to se,
Saying, 'The king of beistis mak I the,
And the cheif protector in woddis and schawis:
Onto thi leigis go furth, and keip the lawis.   105

Exerce justice with mercy and conscience,
And lat no small beist suffir skaith na skornis
Of greit beistis that bene of moir piscence;
Do law elyk to aipis and unicornis,
And lat no bowgle with his busteous hornis   110
The meik pluch ox oppress, for all his pryd,
Bot in the yok go peciable him besyd.'

Quhen this was said, with noyis and soun of joy
All kynd of beistis in to thair degre
At onis cryit lawd, 'Vive le Roy',   115
And till his feit fell with humilite;
And all thay maid him homege and fewte,
And he did thame ressaif with princely laitis,
Quhois noble yre is *parcere prostratis*.

Syne crownit scho the Egle king of fowlis,   120
And as steill dertis scherpit scho his pennis,
And bawd him be als just to awppis and owlis
As unto pacokkis, papingais, or crennis,
And mak a law for wycht fowlis and for wrennis;
And lat no fowll of ravyne do efferay,   125
Nor devoir birdis bot his awin pray.

Than callit scho all flouris that grew on feild,
Discirnyng all thair fassionis and effeiris;
Upon the awfull Thrissill scho beheld
And saw him kepit with a busche of speiris;   130
Concedring him so able for the weiris,
A radius croun of rubeis scho him gaif
And said, 'In feild go furth and fend the laif:

And sen thow art a king, thow be discreit;
Herb without vertew thow hald nocht of sic pryce 135
As herb of vertew and of odor sueit,
And lat no nettill vyle and full of vyce
Hir fallow to the gudly flour delyce,
Nor latt no wyld weid full of churlichenes
Compair hir till the lilleis nobilnes.   140

Nor hald non udir flour in sic denty
As the fresche Ros of cullour reid and quhyt;
For gife thow dois, hurt is thyne honesty,
Conciddering that no flour is so perfyt,
So full of vertew, plesans, and delyt,   145
So full of blisfull angellik bewty,
Imperiall birth, honour and dignite.'

Than to the Ros scho turnyt hir visage
And said, 'O lusty dochtir most benyng,
Aboif the lilly illustare of lynnage,   150
Fro the stok ryell rysing fresche and ying,
But ony spot or macull doing spring;
Cum, blowme of joy, with jemis to be cround,
For our the laif thy bewty is renownd.'

A coistly croun with clarefeid stonis brycht   155
This cumly quene did on hir heid inclois,
Quhill all the land illumynit of the licht:
Quhairfoir me thocht all flouris did rejos,

(14)

Crying attonis, 'Haill be thow richest Ros,
Haill hairbis empryce, haill freschest quene of flouris;
To the be glory and honour at all houris.'   161

Thane all the birdis song with voce on hicht,
Quhois mirthfull soun wes mervelus to heir:
The mavys song, 'Haill Rois most riche and richt,
That dois up flureis undir Phebus speir;   165
Haill plant of yowth, haill princes dochtir deir,
Haill blosome breking out of the blud royall,
Quhois pretius vertew is imperiall.'

The merle scho sang, 'Haill Rois of most delyt,
Haill of all flouris quene and soverane';   170
The lark scho song, 'Haill Rois both reid and quhyt,
Most plesand flour of michty cullouris twane';
The nychtingaill song, 'Haill Naturis suffragene
In bewty, nurtour, and every nobilnes,
In riche array, renown, and gentilnes.'   175

The commoun voce uprais of birdis small
Apone this wys, 'O blissit be the hour
That thow wes chosin to be our principall;
Welcome to be our princes of honour,
Our perle, our plesans and our paramour,   180
Our peax, our play, our plane felicite:
Chryst the conserf frome all adversite.'

Than all the birdis song with sic a schout
That I annone awoilk quhair that I lay,
And with a braid I turnyt me about   185
To se this court, bot all wer went away:
Than up I lenyt, halflingis in affrey,
And thus I wret, as ye haif hard to forrow,
Off lusty May upone the nynt morrow.

(15)

6

BLYTH Aberdeane, thow beriall of all tounis,
　　The lamp of bewtie, bountie, and blythnes;
Unto the heaven [ascendit] thy renoun is
　　Off vertew, wisdome, and of worthines;
　　He nottit is thy name of nobilnes.　　　　　　5
Into the cuming of oure lustie quein,
　　The wall of welth, guid cheir and mirrines,
Be blyth and blisfull, burgh of Aberdein.

And first hir mett the burges of the toun,
　　Richelie arrayit as become thame to be,　　　10
Of quhom they cheset four men of renoun
　　In gounes of velvot, young, abill and lustie,
　　To beir the paill of velves cramase
Abone hir heid, as the custome hes bein.
　　Gryt was the sound of the artelyie:　　　　　15
Be blyth and blisfull, burgh of Aberdein.

Ane fair processioun mett hir at the port
　　In a cap of gold and silk full pleasantlie,
Syne at hir entrie, with many fair disport,
　　Ressaveit hir on streittis lustilie;　　　　　　20
　　Quhair first the salutatioun honorabilly
Of the sweitt Virgin guidlie mycht be seine,
　　The sound of menstrallis blawing to the sky:
Be blyth and blisfull, burgh of Aberdein.

And syne thow gart the orient kingis thrie　　25
　　Offer to Chryst, with benyng reverence,
Gold, sence, and mir, with all humilitie,
　　Schawand him king with most magnificence;
　　Syne quhow the angill, with sword of violence,
Furth of the joy of paradice putt clein　　　　30
　　Adame and Ev for innobedience:
Be blyth and blisfull, burcht of Aberdein.

And syne the Bruce, that evir was bold in stour,
   Thow gart as roy cum rydand under croun,
Richt awfull, strang, and large of portratour,   35
   As nobill, dreidfull, michtie campioun;
   The [nobill Stewarts] syne of great renoun
Thow gart upspring, with branches new and greine,
   Sa gloriouslie, quhill glaidid all the toun:
Be blyth and blisfull, burcht of Aberdein.   40

Syne come thair four and tuentie madinis ying
   All claid in greine of mervelous bewtie,
With hair detressit as threidis of gold did hing,
   With quhyt hattis all browderit rycht brav[elie],
   Playand on timberallis and syngand rycht sweitlie;
That seimlie sort, in ordour weill besein,   46
   Did meit the quein, hir [saluand] reverentlie:
Be blyth and blisfull, burcht of Aberdein.

The streittis war all hung with tapestrie,
   Great was the pres of peopill dwelt about,   50
And pleasant padgeanes playit prattelie;
   The legeis all did to thair lady loutt,
   Quha was convoyed with ane royall routt
Off gryt barrounes and lustie ladyis [schene];
   'Welcum our quein', the commones gaif ane schout:
Be blyth and blisfull, burcht of Aberdein.   56

At hir cumming great was the mirth and joy,
   For at thair croce aboundantlie rane wyne;
Untill hir ludgeing the toun did hir convoy;
   Hir for to treit thai sett thair haill ingyne: 60
   Ane riche present thai did till hir propyne,
Ane costlie coup that large thing wald contene,
   Coverit and full of cunyeitt gold rycht fyne:
Be blyth and blisfull, burcht of Aberdein.

O potent princes, pleasant and preclair,   65
    Great caus thow hes to thank this nobill toun
That for to do the honnour did not spair
    Thair geir, riches, substance, and persoun
    The to ressave on maist fair fasoun:
The for to pleis thay socht all way and mein;   70
    Thairfoir, sa lang as quein thow beiris croun,
Be thankfull to this burcht of Aberdein.

7

RENOWNIT, ryall, right reverend and serene,
    Lord hie tryumphing in wirschip and valoure,
Fro kyngis downe, most Cristin knight and kene,
    Most wyse, most valyeand, moste laureat hie victour,
    Onto the sterris upheyt is thyne honour: 5
In Scotland welcum be thyne excellence
    To king, queyne, lord, clerk, knight and servatour,
Withe glorie and honour, lawde and reverence.

Welcum, in stour most strong, incomparable knight,
    The fame of armys and floure of vassalage;   10
Welcum, in were most worthi, wyse and wight,
    Welcum, the soun of Mars of moste curage;
    Welcum, moste lusti branche of our linnage,
In every realme oure scheild and our defence;
    Welcum, our tendir blude of hie parage,   15
With glorie and honour, lawde and reverence. . . .

Welcum, oure indeficient adjutorie
    That evir our naceoun helpit in thare neyd,
That never saw Scot yit indigent nor sory
    But thou did hym suport with thi gud deid;   20
    Welcum therfor, abufe all livand leid,
Withe us to live and to maik recidence,
    Quhilk never sall sunye for thy saik to bleid;
To quham be honour, lawde and reverence.

Is none of Scotland borne faithfull and kynde,   25
   Bot he of naturall inclinacioune
Dois favour the withe all his hert and mynde,
   Withe fervent, tendir, trew intencioun,
   And wald of inwart hie effectioun,
Bot dreyd of danger, de in thi defence   30
   Or dethe or schame war done to thi persoun:
To quham be honour, lawde and reverence . . .

Hie furius Mars, the god armipotent,
   Rong in the hevin at thyne nativite;
Saturnus doune withe fyry eyn did blent   35
   Throw bludy visar, men manasing to gar de;
   On the fresche Venus keist hir amourouse e;
On the Marcurius furtheyet his eloquence;
   Fortuna Maior did turn hir face on the
With glorie and honour, lawde and reverence.   40

Prynce of fredom and flour of gentilnes,
   Sweyrd of knightheid and choise of chevalry,
This tyme I lefe, for grete prolixitnes,
   To tell quhat feildis thou wan in Pikkardy,
   In France, in Bertan, in Naplis and Lumbardy;   45
As I think eftir, withe all my diligence,
   Or thow departe, at lenthe for to discry
With glorie and honour, lawde and reverence.

B in thi name betaknis batalrus,
   A able in feild, R right renoune most hie,   50
N nobilnes, and A for aunterus,
   R ryall blude, for dughtines is D,
   V valyeantnes, S for strenewite:
Quhoise knyghtli name, so schynyng in clemence,
   For wourthines in gold suld writtin be   55
With glorie and honour, lawde and reverence.

D

8

LANG heff I maed of ladyes quhytt,
Nou of ane blak I will indytt
   That landet furth of the last schippis;
Quhou fain wald I descryve perfytt
   My ladye with the mekle lippis: 5

Quhou schou is tute mowitt lyk ane aep
And lyk a gangarall onto graip,
   And quhou hir schort catt nois up skippis,
And quhou scho schynes lyk ony saep:
   My ladye with the mekle lippis.   10

Quhen schou is claid in reche apparrall
Schou blinkis als brycht as ane tar barrell;
   Quhen schou was born the son tholit clippis,
The nycht be fain faucht in hir querrell:
   My ladye with the mekle lippis.   15

Quhai for hir saek with speir and scheld
Preiffis maest mychttelye in the feld
   Sall kis and withe hir go in grippis,
And fra thyne furth hir luff sall weld:
   My ladye with the mekle lippis.   20

And quhai in felde receaves schaem
And tynis thair his knychtlie naem
   Sall cum behind and kis hir hippis,
And nevir to uther confort claem:
   My ladye with the mekle lippis.   25

9

SWEIT rois of vertew and of gentilnes,
Delytsum lyllie of everie lustynes,
   Richest in bontie and in bewtie cleir,
   And everie vertew that is [held maist] deir,
Except onlie that ye ar mercyles.   5

In to your garthe this day I did persew;
Thair saw I flowris that fresche wer of hew,
   Baith quhyte and reid moist lusty wer to seyne,
   And halsum herbis upone stalkis grene,
Yit leif nor flour fynd could I nane of rew.   10

I dout that Merche with his caild blastis keyne
Hes slane this gentill herbe that I of mene,
   Quhois petewous deithe dois to my hart sic pane
   That I wald mak to plant his rute agane,
So confortand his levis unto me bene.   15

10

SEN that I am a presoneir
Till hir that farest is and best,
I me commend fra yeir till yeir
In till hir bandoun for to rest:
I govit on that gudliest,   5
So lang to luk I tuk laiseir,
Quhill I wes tane withouttin test
And led furth as a presoneir.

Hir sweit having and fresche bewte
Hes wondit me but swerd or lance;
With hir to go commandit me
Ontill the castell of pennance:

(21)

I said, 'Is this your govirnance
To tak men for thair luking heir?'
Bewty sayis, 'Ya schir, perchance   15
Ye be my ladeis presoneir.'

Thai had me bundin to the yet
Quhair Strangenes had bene portar ay,
And in deliverit me thairat,
And in thir termis can thai say,   20
'Do wait, and lat him nocht away':
Quo Strangenes unto the porteir,
'Ontill my lady, I dar lay,
Ye be to pure a presoneir.'

Thai kest me in a deip dungeoun   25
And fetterit me but lok or cheyne;
The capitane, hecht Comparesone,
To luke on me he thocht greit deyne:
Thocht I wes wo I durst nocht pleyne
For he had fetterit mony a feir;   30
With petous voce thus cuth I sene,
'Wo is a wofull presoneir.'

Langour wes weche upoun the wall,
That nevir sleipit bot evir wouke;
Scorne wes bourdour in the hall   35
And oft on me his babill schuke,
Lukand with mony a dengerous luke:
'Quhat is he yone that methis us neir?
Ye be to townage, be this buke,
To be my ladeis presoneir.'   40

Gud Houp rownit in my eir
And bad me baldlie breve a bill;
With Lawlines he suld it beir,
With Fair Schervice send it hir till.
I wouk and wret hir all my will;   45

(22)

Fair Schervice fur withouttin feir,
Sayand till hir with wirdis still,
'Haif pety of your presoneir.'

Than Lawlines to Petie went
And said till hir in termis schort,   50
'Lat we yone presoneir be schent;
Will no man do to us support?
Gar lay ane sege unto yone fort.'
Than Petie said, 'I sall appeir';
Thocht sayis, 'I hecht, cum I ourthort,   55
I houp to lows the presoneir.'

Than to battell thai war arreyit all,
And ay the vawart kepit Thocht;
Lust bar the benner to the wall
And Bissines the grit gyn brocht: 60
Skorne cryis out, sayis, 'Wald ye ocht?'
Lust sayis, 'We wald haif entre heir';
Comparisone sayis, 'That is for nocht;
Ye will nocht wyn the presoneir.'

Thai thairin schup for to defend,   65
And thai thairfurth sailyeit ane hour;
Than Bissines the grit gyn bend,
Straik doun the top of the foir tour:
Comparisone began to lour
And cryit furth, 'I yow requeir   70
Soft and fair, and do favour,
And tak to yow the presoneir.'

Thai fyrit the yettis deliverly
With faggottis wer grit and huge,
And Strangenes quhair that he did ly   75
Wes brint in to the porter luge.
Lustely thay lakit bot a juge,
Sik straikis and stychling wes on steir;
The semeliest wes maid assege
To quhome that he wes presoner.   80

Thrucht Skornes nos thai put a prik;
This he wes banist and gat a blek:
Comparisone wes erdit quik,
And Langour lap and brak his nek:
Thai sailyeit fast, all the fek: 85
Lust chasit my ladeis chalmirleir;
Gud Fame wes drownit in a sek:
Thus ransonit thai the presoneir.

Fra Sklandir hard Lust had undone
His enemeis, [he] him aganis   90
Assemblit ane semely sort full sone,
And rais, and rowttit all the planis:
His cusing in the court remanis,
Bot jalous folkis and geangleiris
And fals Invy, that no thing lanis,   95
Blew out on Luvis presoneir.

Syne Matremony, that nobill king,
Wes grevit, and gadderit ane grit ost,
And all enermit, without lesing,
Chest Sklander to the west se cost.   100
Than wes he and his linege lost,
And Matremony withowttin weir
The band of freindschip hes indost
Betuix Bewty and the presoneir.

Be that of eild wes Gud Famis air   105
And cumyne to continuatioun,
And to the court maid his repair,
Quhair Matremony than woir the crowne.
He gat ane confirmatioun,
All that his modir aucht but weir,   110
And baid still, as it wes resone,
With Bewty and the presoneir.

II

RYGHT as the stern of day begouth to schyne,
Quhen gone to bed war Vesper and Lucyne,
  I raise, and by a rosere did me rest:
Up sprang the goldyn candill matutyne,
With clere depurit bemes cristallyne   5
  Glading the mery foulis in thair nest;
  Or Phebus was in purpur cape revest
Up raise the lark, the hevyns menstrale fyne,
  In May, in till a morrow myrthfullest.

Full angellike thir birdis sang thair houris   10
Within thair courtyns grene, in to thair bouris
  Apparalit quhite and rede wyth blomes suete;
Anamalit was the felde wyth all colouris,
The perly droppis schake in silvir schouris
  Quhill all in balme did branch and levis flete;   15
  To part fra Phebus did Aurora grete,
Hir cristall teris I saw hyng on the flouris,
  Quhilk he for lufe all drank up wyth his hete.

For mirth of May, wyth skippis and wyth hoppis
The birdis sang upon the tender croppis,   20
  With curiouse note, as Venus chapell clerkis;
The rosis yong, new spreding of thair knopis,
War powderit brycht with hevinly beriall droppis;
  Throu bemes rede birnyng as ruby sperkis
  The skyes rang for schoutyng of the larkis;   25
The purpur hevyn, ourscailit in silvir sloppis,
  Ourgilt the treis, branchis, lef, and barkis.

Doune throu the ryce a ryvir ran wyth stremys
So lustily agayn thai lykand lemys
  That all the lake as lamp did leme of licht,   30
Quhilk schadowit all about wyth twynkling glemis,
That bewis bathit war in secund bemys

Throu the reflex of Phebus visage brycht:
On every syde the hegies raise on hicht,
The bank was grene, the bruke was full of bremys,   35
    The stanneris clere as stern in frosty nycht.

The cristall air, the sapher firmament,
The ruby skyes of the orient,
    Kest beriall bemes on emerant bewis grene;
The rosy garth depaynt and redolent   40
With purpur, azure, gold, and goulis gent,
    Arayed was by dame Flora the quene
    So nobily that joy was for to sene;
The roch agayn the rivir resplendent
    As low enlumynit all the leves schene.   45

Quhat throu the mery foulys armony,
And throu the ryveris soune rycht ran me by,
    On Florais mantill I slepit as I lay;
Quhare sone in to my dremes fantasy
I saw approch agayn the orient sky   50
    A saill als quhite as blossum upon spray,
    Wyth merse of gold brycht as the stern of day,
Quhilk tendit to the land full lustily,
    As falcoune swift desyrouse of hir pray.

And hard on burd unto the blomyt medis,   55
Amang the grene rispis and the redis,
    Arrivit sche; quhar fro anone thare landis
Ane hundreth ladyes, lusty in to wedis,
Als fresch as flouris that in May up spredis,
    In kirtillis grene, withoutyn kell or bandis;   60
    Thair brycht hairis hang gletering on the strandis
In tressis clere, wyppit wyth goldyn thredis;
    With pappis quhite and mydlis small as wandis.

Discrive I wald, bot quho coud wele endyte
How all the feldis wyth thai lilies quhite   65

Depaynt war brycht, quhilk to the hevyn did glete?
Noucht thou, Omer, als fair as thou coud wryte,
For all thine ornate stilis so perfyte;
   Nor yit thou, Tullius, quhois lippis suete
   Off rethorike did in to termes flete: 70
Your aureate tongis both bene all to lyte
   For to compile that paradise complete.

Thare saw I Nature and Venus, quene and quene,
The fresch Aurora and lady Flora schene,
   Juno, Appollo, and Proserpyna,   75
Dyane, the goddesse chaste of woddis grene,
My lady Cleo that help of makaris bene,
   Thetes, Pallas, and prudent Minerva,
   Fair feynit Fortune and lemand Lucina:
Thir mychti quenis in crounis mycht be sene,   80
   Wyth bemys blith, bricht as Lucifera.

Thare saw I May, of myrthfull monethis quene,
Betuix Aprile and June, her sistir schene,
   Within the gardyng walking up and doun,
Quham of the foulis gladdith al bedene;   85
Scho was full tender in hir yeris grene:
   Thare saw I Nature present hir a goune
   Rich to behald and nobil of renoune,
Off eviry hew under the hevin that bene
   Depaynt, and broud be gude proporcioun.   90

Full lustily thir ladyes all in fere
Enterit within this park of most plesere,
   Quhare that I lay our helit wyth levis ronk;
The mery foulis, blisfullest of chere,
Salust Nature, me thoucht, on thair manere,   95
   And eviry blome on branch and eke on bonk
   Opnyt and spred thair balmy levis donk,
Full low enclynyng to thair quene so clere,
   Quham of thair nobill norising thay thonk.

Syne to dame Flora on the samyn wyse   100
Thay saluse and thay thank a thousand syse,
     And to dame Venus, lufis mychti quene,
Thay sang ballettis in lufe, as was the gyse,
With amourouse notis lusty to devise,
     As thay that had lufe in thair hertis grene;   105
     Thair hony throtis, opnyt fro the splene,
With werblis suete did perse the hevinly skyes
     Quhill loud resownyt the firmament serene.

Ane othir court thare saw I consequent
Cupide the king, wyth bow in hand ybent   110
     And dredefull arowis grundyn scharp and square;
Thare saw I Mars, the god armypotent,
Aufull and sterne, strong and corpolent;
     Thare saw I crabbit Saturn ald and haire,
     His luke was lyke for to perturb the aire;   115
Thare was Mercurius, wise and eloquent,
     Of rethorike that fand the flouris faire.

Thare was the god of gardingis, Priapus,
Thare was the god of wildernes, Phanus,
     And Janus, god of entree delytable;   120
Thare was the god of fludis, Neptunus,
Thare was the god of wyndis, Eolus,
     With variand luke rycht lyke a lord unstable;
     Thare was Bacus, the gladder of the table;
Thare was Pluto, the elrich incubus   125
     In cloke of grene; his court usit no sable.

And eviry one of thir, in grene arayit,
On harp or lute full merily thai playit,
     And sang ballettis with michty notis clere;
Ladyes to dance full sobirly assayit,   130
Endlang the lusty ryvir so thai mayit,
     Thair observance rycht hevynly was to here:
     Than crap I throu the levis and drew nere,

(28)

Quhare that I was rycht sudaynly affrayit
  All throu a luke, quhilk I have boucht full dere.   135

And schortly for to speke, be lufis quene
I was aspyit; scho bad hir archearis kene
  Go me arrest, and thay no time delayit.
Than ladyes fair lete fall thair mantillis grene:
With bowis big in tressit hairis schene   140
  All sudaynly thay had a felde arayit:
  And yit rycht gretly was I noucht affrayit,
The party was so plesand for to sene:
  A wonder lusty bikkir me assayit.

And first of all, with bow in hand ybent   145
Come dame Beautee, rycht as scho wald me schent;
  Syne folowit all hir dameselis yfere
With mony diverse aufull instrument:
Unto the pres Fair Having wyth hir went,
  Fyne Portrature, Plesance, and lusty Chere.   150
  Than come Resoun with schelde of gold so clere,
In plate and maille, as Mars armypotent,
Defendit me that nobil chevallere.

Syne tender Youth come wyth hir virgyns ying,
Grene Innocence, and schamefull Abaising,   155
  And quaking Drede wyth humble Obedience:
The goldyn targe harmyt thay no thing,
Curage in thame was noucht begonne to spring;
  Full sore thay dred to done a violence.
  Suete Womanhede I saw cum in presence;   160
Of artilye a warld sche did in bring,
  Servit wyth ladyes full of reverence.

Sche led wyth hir Nurture and Lawlynes,
Contenence, Pacience, Gude Fame, and Stedfastnes,
  Discrecioun, Gentrise, and Considerance,   165
Levefell Company and Honest Besynes,

Benigne Luke, Mylde Chere, and Sobirnes.
    All thir bure ganyeis to do me grevance;
    But Resoun bure the targe wyth sik constance,
Thair scharp assayes mycht do no dures   170
    To me, for all thair aufull ordynance.

Unto the pres persewit Hie Degree;
Hir folowit ay Estate and Dignitee,
    Comparisoun, Honour and Noble Array,
Will, Wantonnes, Renoun, and Libertee,   175
Richesse, Fredome, and eke Nobilitee:
    Wit ye thay did thair baner hye display;
    A cloud of arowis as hayle schour lousit thay,
And schot quhill wastit was thair artilye,
    Syne went abak, reboytit of thair pray.   180

Quhen Venus had persavit this rebute,
Dissymilance scho bad go mak persute,
    At all powere to perse the goldyn targe;
And scho, that was of doubilnes the rute,
Askit hir choise of archeris in refute.   185
    Venus the best bad hir go wale at large;
    Scho tuke Presence, plicht anker of the barge,
And Fair Callyng that wele a flayn coud schute,
    And Cherising for to complete hir charge.

Dame Hamelynes scho tuke in company,   190
That hardy was and hende in archery,
    And broucht dame Beautee to the felde agayn
With all the choise of Venus chevalry;
Thay come and bikkerit unabaisitly:
    The schour of arowis rappit on as rayn;   195
    Perilouse Presence, that mony syre has slayne,
The bataill broucht on bordour hard us by;
    The salt was all the sarar, suth to sayn.

(30)

Thik was the schote of grundyn dartis kene;
Bot Resoun with the scheld of gold so schene   200
    Warly defendit quho so evir assayit:
The aufull stoure he manly did sustene
Quhill Presence kest a pulder in his ene,
    And than as drunkyn man he all forvayit.
    Quhen he was blynd, the fule wyth hym thay playit, 205
And banyst hym amang the bewis grene:
    That sory sicht me sudaynly affrayit.

Than was I woundit to the deth wele nere,
And yoldyn as a wofull prisonnere
    To lady Beautee in a moment space;   210
Me thoucht scho semyt lustiar of chere,
Efter that Resoun tynt had his eyne clere,
    Than of before, and lufliare of face;
    Quhy was thou blyndit, Resoun, quhi, allace:
And gert ane hell my paradise appere,   215
    And mercy seme, quhare that I fand no grace?

Dissymulance was besy me to sile,
And Fair Calling did oft apon me smyle,
    And Cherising me fed wyth wordis fair;
New Acquyntance enbracit me a quhile   220
And favouryt me, quhill men mycht go a myle,
    Syne tuk hir leve; I saw hir nevir mare.
    Than saw I Dangere toward me repair;
I coud eschew hir presence be no wyle.
    On syde scho lukit wyth ane fremyt fare,   225

And at the last, departing coud hir dresse,
And me delyverit unto Hevynesse
    For to remayne, and scho in cure me tuke.
Be this the lord of wyndis, wyth wodenes,
God Eolus, his bugill blew, I gesse,   230

That with the blast the levis all to-schuke;
And sudaynly in the space of a luke
    All was hyne went, thare was bot wildernes,
    Thare was no more bot birdis, bank, and bruke.

In twynkling of ane eye to schip thai went,   235
And swyth up saile unto the top thai stent,
    And with swift course atour the flude thay frak;
Thay fyrit gunnis wyth powder violent
Till that the reke raise to the firmament;
    The rochis all resownyt wyth the rak,   240
    For rede it semyt that the raynbow brak;
Wyth spirit affrayde apon my fete I sprent,
    Amang the clewis so carefull was the crak.

And as I did awake of my sueving,
The joyfull birdis merily did syng   245
    For myrth of Phebus tendir bemes schene;
Suete war the vapouris, soft the morowing,
Halesum the vale depaynt wyth flouris ying,
    The air attemperit, sobir and amene;
    In quhite and rede was all the felde besene   250
Throu Naturis nobil fresch anamalyng,
    In mirthfull May, of eviry moneth Quene.

O reverend Chaucere, rose of rethoris all,
As in oure tong ane flour imperiall,
    That raise in Britane evir, quho redis rycht,   255
Thou beris of makaris the tryumph riall;
Thy fresch anamalit termes celicall
    This mater coud illumynit have full brycht:
    Was thou noucht of oure Inglisch all the lycht,
Surmounting eviry tong terrestriall   260
    Alls fer as Mayis morow dois mydnycht?

O morall Gower, and Ludgate laureate,
Your sugurit lippis and tongis aureate

Bene to oure eris cause of grete delyte;
Your angel mouthis most mellifluate 265
Oure rude langage has clere illumynate,
   And fair ourgilt oure speche, that imperfyte
   Stude, or your goldyn pennis schupe to wryte:
This ile before was bare and desolate
   Off rethorike or lusty fresch endyte. 270

Thou lytill quair, be evir obedient,
Humble, subject, and symple of entent
   Before the face of eviry connyng wicht:
I knaw quhat thou of rethorike hes spent;
Off all hir lusty rosis redolent 275
   Is none in to thy gerland sett on hicht;
   Eschame thar of and draw the out of sicht.
Rude is thy wede, disteynit, bare, and rent;
   Wele aucht thou be aferit of the licht.

12

APON the Midsummer evin, mirriest of nichtis,
I muvit furth allane neir as midnicht wes past,
Besyd ane gudlie grein garth, full of gay flouris,
Hegeit of ane huge hicht with hawthorne treis,
Quhairon ane bird on ane bransche so birst out hir notis 5
That never ane blythfullar bird was on the beuchè harde.
Quhat throw the sugarat sound of hir sang glaid,
And throw the savour sanative of the sueit flouris,
I drew in derne to the dyk to dirkin efter mirthis.
The dew donkit the daill, and dynnit the feulis. 10
   I hard, under ane holyn hevinlie grein hewit,
Ane hie speiche at my hand, with hautand wourdis;
With that in haist to the hege so hard I inthrang
That I was heildit with hawthorne and with heynd leveis:
Throw pykis of the plet thorne I presandlie luikit, 15
Gif ony persoun wald approche within that plesand garding.

I saw thre gay ladeis sit in ane grene arbeir,
All grathit in to garlandis of fresche gudlie flouris:
So glitterit as the gold wer thair glorius gilt tressis,
Quhill all the gressis did gleme of the glaid hewis;   20
Kemmit was thair cleir hair, and curiouslie sched
Attour thair schulderis doun schyre, schyning full bricht,
With curches cassin thair abone of kirsp cleir and thin.
Thair mantillis grein war as the gress that grew in May
      sessoun,
Fetrit with thair quhyt fingaris about thair fair sydis.   25
Off ferliful fyne favour war thair faceis meik,
All full of flurist fairheid as flouris in June,
Quhyt, seimlie, and soft, as the sweit lillies
New upspred upon spray, as new spynist rose;
Arrayit ryallie about with mony riche vardour,   30
That Nature full nobillie annamalit with flouris
Off alkin hewis under hevin that ony heynd knew,
Fragrant, all full of fresche odour fynest of smell.
Ane cumlie tabil coverit wes befoir tha cleir ladeis,
With ryalle cowpis apon rawis full of ryche wynis.   35
And of thir fair wlonkes, tua weddit war with lordis;
Ane wes ane wedow, I wis, wantoun of laitis.
And, as thai talk at the tabill of many taill sindry,
Thay wauchtit at the wicht wyne and waris out wourdis,
And syne thai spak more spedelie and sparit no matiris. 40
  'Bewrie,' said the wedo, 'ye woddit wemen ying,
Quhat mirth ye fand in maryage sen ye war menis wyffis:
Reveill gif ye rewit that rakles conditioun,
Or gif that ever ye luffit leyd upone lyf mair
Nor thame that ye your fayth hes festinit for ever;   45
Or gif ye think, had ye chois, that ye wald cheis better.
Think ye it nocht ane blist band that bindis so fast
That none undo it a deill may bot the deith ane?'

  Than spak ane lusty belyf with lustie effeiris:
'It that ye call the blist band that bindis so fast   50

(34)

Is bair of blis, and bailfull, and greit barrat wirkis.
Ye speir, had I fre chois, gif I wald cheis better:
Chenyeis ay ar to eschew, and changeis ar sueit.
Sic cursit chance till eschew, had I my chois anis,
Out of the chenyeis of ane churle I chaip suld for evir.   55
God gif matrimony were made to mell for ane yeir!
It war bot merrens to be mair, bot gif our myndis pleisit:
It is agane the law of luf, of kynd, and of nature,
Togiddir hairtis to strene that stryveis with uther;
Birdis hes ane better law na bernis, be meikill,   60
That ilk yeir with new joy joyis ane maik,
And fangis thame ane fresche feyr, unfulyeit and constant,
And lattis thair fulyeit feiris flie quhair thai pleis.
Cryst gif sic ane consuetude war in this kith haldin!
Than weill war us wemen that evir we war fre,   65
We suld have feiris as fresche to fang quhen us likit,
And gif all larbaris thair leveis quhen thai lak curage.
My self suld be full semlie in silkis arrayit,
Gymp, jolie and gent, richt joyus and gent;
I suld at fairis be found new faceis to se,   70
At playis, and at preichingis and pilgrimages greit,
To schaw my renone royaly, quhair preis was of folk,
To manifest my makdome to multitude of pepill,
And blaw my bewtie on breid quhair bernis war mony,
That I micht cheis and be chosin, and change quhen me
    lykit . . .   75
    I have ane wallidrag, ane worme, ane auld wobat carle,
A waistit wolroun, na worth bot wourdis to clatter,
Ane bumbart, ane dron bee, ane bag full of flewme,
Ane skabbit skarth, ane scorpioun, ane scutarde behind;
To see him scart his awin skyn grit scunner ι think . . . 80
With goreis his tua grim ene ar gladderrit all about,
And gorgeit lyk twa gutaris that war with glar stoppit;
Bot quhen that glowrand gaist grippis me about,
Than think I hiddowus Mahowne hes me in armes;
Thair ma na sanyne me save fra that auld Sathane,   85

For thocht I croce me all cleine fra the croun doun,
He wil my corse all beclip and clap me to his breist.
Quhen schaiffyne is that ald schalk with a scharp rasour
He schowis one me his schevill mouth and schedis my lippis,
And with his hard hurcheone skyn sa heklis he my chekis 90
That as a glemand gleyd glowis my chaftis;
I schrenk for the scharp stound, bot schout dar I nought
For schore of that auld schrew, schame him betide.
The luf blenkis of that bogill fra his blerde ene,
As Belzebub had on me blent, abasit my spreit. . . . 95

Onone, quhen this amyable had endit hir speche,
Loudly lauchand the laif allowit hir mekle.
Thir gay wiffis maid game amang the grene leiffis;
Thai drank and did away dule under derne bewis;
Thai swapit of the sueit wyne, thai swanquhit of hewis, 100
Bot all the pertlyar in plane thai put out ther vocis.
    Than said the weido, 'iwis, ther is no way othir;
Now tydis me for to talk, my taill it is nixt.
God my spreit now inspir and my speche quykkin,
And send me sentence to say, substantious and noble, 105
Sa that my preching may pers your perverst hertis,
And mak yow mekar to men in maneris and conditiounis.
    I schaw yow, sisteris in schrift, I wes a schrew evir,
Bot I wes schene in my schrowd and schew me innocent;
And thought I dour wes and dane, dispitous and bald, 110
I wes dissymblit suttelly in a sanctis liknes:
I semyt sober and sueit, and sempill without fraud,
Bot I couth sexty dissaif that suttillar wer haldin.
    Unto my lesson ye lyth, and leir at me wit,
Gif you nought list be forleit with losingeris untrew: 115
Be constant in your governance and counterfeit gud maneris,
Thought ye be kene, inconstant, and cruell of mynd;
Thought ye as tygris be terne, be tretable in luf,
And be as turtoris in your talk thought ye haif talis brukill;
Be dragonis baith and dowis ay in double forme, 120

(36)

And quhen it nedis yow, onone, note baith ther strenthis;
Be amyable with humble face, as angellis apperand,
And with a terrebill taill be stangand as edderis;
Be of your luke like innocentis, thoght ye haif evill myndis,
Be courtly ay in clething and costly arrayit: 125
That hurtis yow nought worth a hen; yowr husband pays for
        all.

    Twa husbandis haif I had; thai held me baith deir:
Thought I dispytit thaim agane thai spyit it na thing.
Ane wes ane hair hogeart that hostit out flewme;
I hatit him like a hund, thought I it hid preve.   130
With kissing and with clapping I gert the carll fone;
Weil couth I claw his cruke bak, and kemm his cowit noddill,
And with a bukky in my cheik bo on him behind,
And with a bek gang about and bler his ald e,
And with a kynd contynance kys his crynd chekis;   135
In to my mynd makand mokis at that mad fader,
Trowand me with trew lufe to treit him so fair.
This cought I do without dule, and na dises tak,
Bot ay be mery in my mynd and myrth full of cher.

    I had a lufsummar leid my lust for to slokyn,   140
That couth be secrete and sure, and ay saif my honour,
And sew bot at certayne tymes and in sicir placis;
Ay when the ald did me anger with akword wordis,
Apon the galland for to goif it gladit me agane.
I had sic wit that for wo weipit I litill,   145
Bot leit the sueit ay the sour to gud sesone bring.
Quhen that the chuf wald me chid with girnand chaftis,
I wald him chuk, cheik and chyn, and cheris him so mekill,
That his cheif chymys [I] had chevist to my sone,
Suppos the churll wes gane chaist or the child wes gottin. 150
As wis woman ay I wrought and not as wod fule,
For mar with wylis I wan na wichtnes of handis.

    Syne maryit I a marchand, myghti of gudis.
He was a man of myd eld and of mene statur;
Bot we na fallowis wer in frendschip or blud,   155

In fredome, na furth bering, na fairnes of persoune;
Quhilk ay the fule did foryhet, for febilnes of knawlege,
Bot I sa oft thoght him on quhill angrit his hert,
And quhilum I put furth my voce and pedder him callit.
I wald ryght tuichandly talk be I wes tuyse maryit,   160
For endit wes my innocence with my ald husband:
I wes apperand to be pert within perfit eild,
Sa sais the curat of our kirk, that knew me full ying.
He is our famous to be fals, that fair worthy prelot,
I salbe laith to lat him le, quhill I may luke furth.   165
I gert the buthman obey, ther wes no bute ellis;
He maid me ryght hie reverens, fra he my rycht knew:
For thocht I say it my self, the severance wes mekle
Betuix his bastard blude and my birth noble.
That page wes never of sic price for to presome anys   170
Unto my persone to be peir, had pete nought grantit:
Bot mercy in to womanheid is a mekle vertu,
For never bot in a gentill hert is generit ony ruth . . . .
   Adew dolour, adew; my daynte now begynis:
Now am I a wedow, iwise, and weill am at ese.   175
I weip as I were woful, but wel is me for ever;
I busk as I wer bailfull, bot blith is my hert.
My mouth it makis murnyng, and my mynd lauchis;
My clokis thai ar caerfull in colour of sabill,
Bot courtly and ryght curyus my corse is ther undir;   180
I drup with a ded luke in my dule habit,
As with manis daill [I] had done for dayis of my lif.
Quhen that I go to the kirk, cled in cair wed,
As foxe in a lambis fleise fenye I my cheir;
Than lay I furght my bright buke one breid one my kne   185
With mony lusty letter ellummynit with gold,
And drawis my clok forthwart our my face quhit
That I may spy, unaspyit, a space me beside;
Full oft I blenk by my buke and blynis of devotioun,
To se quhat berne is best brand, or bredest in schulderis,   190
Or forgeit is maist forcely to furnyse a bancat

In Venus chalmer valyeandly, withoutin vane ruse.
And as the new mone all pale, oppressit with change,
Kythis quhilis her cleir face through cluddis of sable,
So keik I through my clokis, and castis kynd lukis   195
To knychtis, and to cleirkis, and cortly personis . . .
   Bot yit me think the best bourd, quhen baronis and
      knychtis
And othir bachilleris, blith blumyng in youth,
And all my luffaris lele, my lugeing persewis,
And fyllis me wyne wantonly, with weilfair and joy: 200
Sum rownis, and sum ralyeis, and sum redis ballatis;
Sum raiffis furght rudly with riatus speche;
Sum plenis and sum prayis, sum prasis mi bewte,
Sum kissis me, sum clappis me, sum kyndnes me proferis . . .
Bot with my fair calling I comfort thaim all: 205
For he that sittis me nixt, I nip on his finger;
I serf him on the tothir syde on the samin fasson,
And he that behind me sittis, I hard on him lene;
And him befor, with my fut fast on his I stramp;
And to the bernis far but sueit blenkis I cast: 210
To every man in speciall speke I sum wordis
So wisly and so womanly, quhill warmys ther hertis.
   Thar is no liffand leid so law of degre
That sall me luf unluffit, I am so loik hertit;
And gif his lust so be lent into my lyre quhit   215
That he be lost or with me lig, his lif sall nocht danger.
I am so mercifull in mynd, and menys all wichtis,
My sely saull salbe saif quhen sa [God] all jugis.
Ladyis, leir thir lessonis, and be no lassis fundin;
This is the legeand of my lif, thought Latyne it be nane.'   220
   Quhen endit had her ornat speche this eloquent wedow,
Lowd thai lewch all the laif, and loffit her mekle,
And said thai suld exampill tak of her soverane teching
And wirk efter hir wordis, that woman wes so prudent.
Than culit thai thair mouthis with confortable drinkis,   225
And carpit full cummerlik with cop going round.

Thus draif thai our that deir nyght with danceis full noble,
Quhill that the day did up daw and dew donkit flouris.
The morow myld wes and meik, the mavis did sing,
And all remuffit the myst, and the meid smellit;   230
Silver schouris doune schuke as the schene cristall,
And berdis schoutit in schaw with thair schill notis;
The goldin glitterand gleme so gladit ther hertis,
Thai maid a glorius gle amang the grene bewis.
The soft sowch of the swyr and soune of the stremys,   235
The sueit savour of the sward and singing of foulis,
Myght confort ony creatur of the kyn of Adam
And kindill agane his curage, thocht it wer cald sloknyt.
Than rais thir ryall roisis in ther riche wedis,
And rakit hame to ther rest through the rise blumys;   240
And I all prevely past to a plesand arber,
And with my pen did report thair pastance most mery.

Ye auditoris most honorable, that eris has gevin
Oneto this uncouth aventur quhilk airly me happinnit:
Of thir thre wantoun wiffis that I haif writtin heir,   245
Quhilk wald ye waill to your wif, gif ye suld wed one?

13

IN secreit place this hyndir nycht
I hard ane beyrne say till ane bricht,
'My huny, my hart, my hoip, my heill,
I have bene lang your luifar leill
And can of yow get confort nane: 5
How lang will ye with danger deill?
Ye brek my hart, my bony ane.'

His bony beird was kemmit and croppit,
Bot all with cale it was bedroppit,
And he wes townysche, peirt and gukit.   10

He clappit fast, he kist and chukkit
As with the glaikis he wer ouirgane;
Yit be his feirris he wald have fukkit:
'Ye brek my hart, my bony ane.'

Quod he, 'My hairt, sweit as the hunye,   15
Sen that I borne wes of my mynnye
I never wowit weycht bot yow;
My wambe is of your luif sa fow
That as ane gaist I glour and grane,
I trymble sa, ye will not trow: 20
Ye brek my hart, my bony ane.'

'Tehe', quod scho, and gaif ane gawfe;
'Be still my tuchan and my calfe,
My new spanit howffing fra the sowk,
And all the blythnes of my bowk;   25
My sweit swanking, saif yow allane
Na leid I luiffit all this owk:
Full leifis me your graceles gane.'

Quod he, 'My claver and my curldodie,
My huny soppis, my sweit possodie,   30
Be not oure bosteous to your billie,
Be warme hairtit and not evill willie;
Your heylis quhyt as quhalis bane,
Garris ryis on loft my quhillelillie:
Ye brek my hart, my bony ane.'   35

Quod scho, 'My clype, my unspaynit gyane
With moderis mylk yit in your mychane,
My belly huddrun, my swete hurle bawsy,
My huny gukkis, my slawsy gawsy,
Your musing waild perse ane hart of stane: 40
Tak gud confort, my grit heidit slawsy,
Full leifis me your graceles gane.'

(41)

Quod he, 'My kid, my capirculyoun,
My bony baib with the ruch brylyoun,
My tendir gyrle, my wallie gowdye,   45
My tyrlie myrlie, my crowdie mowdie,
Quhone that oure mouthis dois meit at ane
My stang dois storkyn with your towdie:
Ye brek my hairt, my bony ane.'

Quod scho, 'Now tak me be the hand,   50
Welcum, my golk of Marie land,
My chirrie and my maikles munyoun,
My sowklar sweit as ony unyoun,
My strumill stirk yit new to spane,
I am applyit to your opunyoun: 55
I luif rycht weill your graceles gane.'

He gaiff to hir ane apill rubye;
Quod scho, 'Gramercye, my sweit cowhubye'.
And thai tway to ane play began
Quhilk men dois call the dery dan,   60
Quhill that thair myrthis met baythe in ane:
'Wo is me', quod scho, 'Quhair will ye, man?
Best now I luif that graceles gane.'

14

THIS nycht befoir the dawing cleir
Me thocht Sanct Francis did to me appeir
With ane religious abbeit in his hand,
And said, 'In this go cleith the, my servand;
Reffus the warld, for thow mon be a freir.'   5

With him and with his abbeit bayth I skarrit,
Lyk to ane man that with a gaist wes marrit;
Me thocht on bed he layid it me abone,
Bot on the flure delyverly and sone
I lap thairfra, and nevir wald cum nar it.   10

Quoth he, 'Quhy skarris thow with this holy weid?
Cleith the thairin, for weir it thow most neid;
Thow that hes lang done Venus lawis teiche
Sall now be freir, and in this abbeit preiche;
Delay it nocht, it mon be done but dreid.   15

My brethir oft hes maid the supplicationis
Be epistillis, sermonis, and relationis,
To tak the abyte, bot thow did postpone;
But ony proces, cum on thairfoir annone,
All sircumstance put by, and excusationis.'   20

Quod I, 'Sanct Francis, loving be the till,
And thankit mot thow be of thy gude will
To me, that of thy clayis ar so kynd,
Bot thame to weir it nevir come in my mynd;
Sweit Confessour, thow tak it nocht in ill.   25

In haly legendis haif I hard allevin
Ma sanctis of bischoppis nor freiris, be sic sevin;

Off full few freiris that hes bene sanctis I reid:
Quhairfoir ga bring to me ane bischopis weid,
Gife evir thow wald my sawle gaid unto hevin.   30

Gif evir my fortoun wes to be a freir,
The dait thairof is past full mony a yeir;
For into every lusty toun and place
Off all Yngland, frome Berwick to Kalice,
I haif in to thy habeit maid gud cheir.   35

In freiris weid full fairly haif I fleichit,
In it haif I in pulpet gon and preichit
In Derntoun kirk and eik in Canterberry;
In it I past at Dover our the ferry
Throw Piccardy, and thair the peple teichit.   40

Als lang as I did beir the freiris style,
In me, God wait, wes mony wrink and wyle;
In me wes falset with every wicht to flatter,
Quhilk mycht be flemit with na haly watter;
I wes ay reddy all men to begyle.'   45

This freir that did Sanct Francis thair appeir,
Ane fieind he wes in liknes of ane freir;
He vaneist away with stynk and fyrie smowk:
With him me thocht all the hous end he towk,
And I awoik as wy that wes in weir.   50

15

As yung Awrora with cristall haile
In orient schew hir visage paile,
A swevyng swyth did me assaile
   Off sonis of Sathanis seid:
Me thocht a Turk of Tartary   5
Come throw the boundis of Barbary,
And lay forloppin in Lumbardy
   Full lang in waithman weid.

Fra baptasing for to eschew,
Thair a religious man he slew   10
And cled him in his abeit new,
   For he cowth wryte and reid.
Quhen kend was his dissimulance
And all his cursit govirnance,
For feir he fled and come in France   15
   With littill of Lumbard leid.
To be a leiche he fenyt him thair,
Quhilk mony a man micht rew evirmair,
For he left nowthir seik nor sair
   Unslane, or he hyne yeid.   20
Vane organis he full clenely carvit;
Quhen of his straik so mony starvit,
Dreid he had gottin that he desarvit;
   He fled away gud speid.

In Scotland than the narrest way   25
He come his cunnyng till assay,
To sum man thair it was no play,
   The preving of his sciens.
In pottingry he wrocht grit pyne,
He murdreist mony in medecyne,   30
The jow was of a grit engyne
   And generit was of gyans.
In leichecraft he was homecyd;
He wald haif, for a nicht to byd,
A haiknay and the hurt manis hyd,   35
   So meikle he was of myance.
His yrnis was rude as ony rawchtir,
Quhair he leit blude it was no lawchtir;
Full mony instrument for slawchtir
   Was in his gardevyance.   40

He cowth gif cure for laxatyve
To gar a wicht hors want his lyve;

Quha evir assay wald, man or wyve,
   Thair hippis yeid hiddy giddy.
His practikis nevir war put to preif   45
But suddane deid or grit mischeif;
He had purgatioun to mak a theif
   To dee withowt a widdy.
Unto no mes pressit this prelat
For sound of sacring bell nor skellat;   50
As blaksmyth bruikit was his pallatt
  For battering at the study.
Thocht he come hame a new maid channoun
He had dispensit with matynnis cannoun,
On him come nowther stole nor fannoun   55
   For smowking of the smydy.

Me thocht seir fassonis he assailyeit
To mak the quintessance, and failyeit,
And quhen he saw that nocht availyeit
   A fedrem on he tuke,   60
And schupe in Turky for to fle;
And quhen that he did mount on he,
All fowill ferleit quhat he sowld be
   That evir did on him luke.
Sum held he had bene Dedalus,   65
Sum the Menatair marvelus,
Sum Martis blaksmyth Vulcanus,
   And sum Saturnus kuke.
And evir the cuschettis at him tuggit,
The rukis him rent, the ravynis him druggit,   70
The hudit crawis his hair furth ruggit;
   The hevin he micht not bruke.

The myttane and Sanct Martynis fowle
Wend he had bene the hornit howle;
Thay set aupone him with a yowle   75
   And gaif him dynt for dynt.
The golk, the gormaw, and the gled

Beft him with buffettis quhill he bled;
The sparhalk to the spring him sped
   Als fers as fyre of flynt.   80
The tarsall gaif him tug for tug,
A stanchell hang in ilka lug,
The pyot furth his pennis did rug,
   The stork straik ay but stynt.
The bissart, bissy but rebuik,   85
Scho was so cleverus of hir cluik,
His bawis he micht not langer bruik:
   Scho held thame at ane hint.

Thik was the clud of kayis and crawis,
Of marleyonis, mittanis, and of mawis,   90
That bikkrit at his berd with blawis
   In battell him abowt.
Thay nybbillit him with noyis and cry,
The rerd of thame rais to the sky,
And evir he cryit on Fortoun, Fy;   95
   His lyfe was in to dowt.
The ja him skrippit with a skryke
And skornit him as it was lyk,
The egill strong at him did stryke
   And rawcht him mony a rowt.   100
For feir uncunnandly he cawkit
Quhill all his pennis war drownd and drawkit;
He maid a hundreth nolt all hawkit
   Beneth him with a spowt.

He schewre his feddreme that was schene   105
And slippit owt of it full clene,
And in a myre up to the ene
   Amang the glar did glyd.
The fowlis all at the fedrem dang
As at a monster thame amang,   110
Quhill all the pennis of it owsprang
   In till the air full wyde.

And he lay at the plunge evirmair
So lang as any ravin did rair,
The crawis him socht with cryis of cair   115
    In every schaw besyde.
Had he reveild bene to the ruikis
Thay had him revin all with thair cluikis;
Thre dayis in dub amang the dukis
    He did with dirt him hyde.   120
The air was dirkit with the fowlis
That come with yawmeris and with yowlis,
With skryking, skrymming, and with scowlis,
    To tak him in the tyde.
I walknit with the noyis and schowte,   125
So hiddowis beir was me abowte;
Sensyne I curs that cankerit rowte
    Quhair evir I go or ryde.

16

Lucina schynnyng in silence of the nicht,
The hevin being all full of sternis bricht,
To bed I went, bot thair I tuke no rest;
With havy thocht I wes so soir opprest
That sair I langit eftir dayis licht.   5

Off Fortoun I complenit hevely,
That scho to me stude so contrariowsly;
And at the last, quhen I had turnyt oft,
For weirines on me ane slummer soft
Come with ane dremyng and a fantesy.   10

Me thocht deme Fortoun with ane fremmit cheir
Stude me beforne and said on this maneir,
'Thow suffer me to wirk gif thow do weill
And preis the nocht to stryfe aganis my quheill,
Quhilk every wardly thing dois turne and steir.   15

Full mony ane man I turne unto the hicht,
And makis als mony full law to doun licht;
Up on my staigis or that thow ascend,
Trest weill thy truble neir is at ane end,
Seing thir taikinis; quhairfoir thow mark thame rycht: 20

Thy trublit gaist sall neir moir be degest,
Nor thow in to no benifice beis possest,
Quhill that ane abbot him cleith in ernis pennis
And fle up in the air amangis the crennis,
And as ane falcone fair fro eist to west.   25

He sall ascend as ane horrebble grephoun,
Him meit sall in the air ane scho dragoun;
Thir terrible monsteris sall togidder thrist
And in the cludis gett the Antechrist,
Quhill all the air infeck of thair pusoun.   30

Under Saturnus fyrie regioun
Symone Magus sall meit him, and Mahoun;
And Merlyne at the mone sall him be bydand,
And Jonet the weido on ane bussome rydand,
Off wichis with ane windir garesoun.   35

And syne thay sall discend with reik and fyre,
And preiche in erth the Antechrysts impyre;
Be than it salbe neir this warldis end.'
With that this lady sone fra me did wend;
Sleipand and walkand wes frustrat my desyre.   40

Quhen I awoik, my dreme it wes so nyce,
Fra every wicht I hid it as a vyce,
Quhill I hard tell be mony suthfast wy
Fle wald ane abbot up in to the sky,
And all his fethreme maid wes at devyce.   45

Within my hairt confort I tuke full sone;
'Adew', quod I, 'My drery dayis ar done';
Full weill I wist to me wald nevir cum thrift
Quhill that twa monis wer sene up in the lift,
Or quhill ane abbot flew aboif the mone.   50

17

OFF Februar the fyiftene nycht
Full lang befoir the dayis lycht
   I lay in till a trance;
And then I saw baith hevin and hell:
Me thocht amangis the feyndis fell   5
   Mahoun gart cry ane dance
Off schrewis that wer nevir schrevin,
Aganis the feist of Fasternis evin
   To mak thair observance:
He bad gallandis ga graith a gyis,   10
And kast up gamountis in the skyis
   That last came out of France.

'Lat se', quod he, 'Now quha begynnis?'
With that the fowll sevin deidly synnis
   Begowth to leip at anis.   15
And first of all in dance wes Pryd,
With hair wyld bak and bonet on syd
   Lyk to mak waistie wanis;
And round abowt him as a quheill
Hang all in rumpillis to the heill   20
   His kethat for the nanis.
Mony prowd trumpour with him trippit;
Throw skaldand fyre ay as thay skippit
   Thay gyrnd with hiddous granis.

Heilie harlottis on hawtane wyis   25
Come in with mony sindrie gyis,
   Bot yit luche nevir Mahoun

Quhill preistis come in with bair schevin nekkis:
Than all the feyndis lewche and maid gekkis,
    Blak Belly and Bawsy Brown.   30

Than Yre come in with sturt and stryfe,
His hand wes ay upoun his knyfe,
    He brandeist lyk a beir;
Bostaris, braggaris, and barganeris
Eftir him passit in to pairis,   35
    All bodin in feir of weir,
In jakkis and stryppis and bonettis of steill;
Thair leggis wer chenyeit to the heill,
    Frawart wes thair affeir;
Sum upoun udir with brandis beft,   40
Sum jaggit uthiris to the heft
    With knyvis that scherp cowd scheir.

Nixt in the dance followit Envy,
Fild full of feid and fellony,
    Hid malyce and dispyte;   45
For pryvie hatrent that tratour trymlit;
Him followit mony freik dissymlit
    With fenyeit wirdis quhyte,
And flattereris in to menis facis
And bakbyttaris in secreit placis   50
    To ley that had delyte,
And rownaris of fals lesingis:
Allace, that courtis of noble kingis
    Of thame can nevir be quyte.

Nixt him in dans come Cuvatyce,   55
Rute of all evill and grund of vyce,
    That nevir cowd be content;
Catyvis, wrechis, and ockeraris,
Hud pykis, hurdaris, and gadderaris—
    All with that warlo went: 60

Out of thair throttis thay schot on udder
Hett moltin gold, me thocht a fudder,
   As fyreflawcht maist fervent;
Ay as thay tomit thame of schot
Feyndis fild thame new up to the thrott   65
   With gold of allkin prent.

Syne Sweirnes, at the secound bidding,
Come lyk a sow out of a midding,
   Full slepy wes his grunyie;
Mony sweir bumbard belly huddroun,   70
Mony slute daw and slepy duddroun,
   Him servit ay with sounyie:
He drew thame furth in till a chenyie,
And Belliall with a brydill renyie
   Evir lascht thame on the lunyie;   75
In dance thay war so slaw of feit
Thay gaif thame in the fyre a heit
   And maid thame quicker of counyie.

Than Lichery that lathly cors
Come berand lyk a bagit hors,   80
   And Ydilnes did him leid;
Thair wes with him ane ugly sort,
And mony stynkand fowll tramort
   That had in syn bene deid:
Quhen thay wer entrit in the dance   85
Thay wer full strenge of countenance,
   Lyk turkas birnand reid;
All led thay uthir by the tersis,
Suppois thay fycket with thair ersis
   It mycht be na remeid.   90

Than the fowll monstir Glutteny,
Off wame unsasiable and gredy,
   To dance he did him dres;
Him followit mony fowll drunckart

With can and collep, cop and quart,   95
    In surffet and exces;
Full mony a waistles wallydrag
With wamis unweildable did furth wag
    In creische that did incres.
'Drynk', ay thay cryit with mony a gaip;   100
The feyndis gaif thame hait leid to laip,
    Thair lovery wes na les.
Na menstrallis playit to thame but dowt,
For glemen thair wer haldin owt
    Be day and eik by nycht: 105
Except a menstrall that slew a man,
Swa till his heretage he wan
    And entirt be breif of richt.

Than cryd Mahoun for a heleand padyane;
Syne ran a feynd to feche Makfadyane   110
    Far northwart in a nuke:
Be he the correnoch had done schout,
Erschemen so gadderit him abowt,
    In hell grit rowme thay tuke.
Thae tarmegantis, with tag and tatter,   115
Full lowd in Ersche begowth to clatter
    And rowp lyk revin and ruke.
The Devill sa devit wes with thair yell,
That in the depest pot of hell
    He smorit thame with smuke.   120

                        18

    N IX T that a turnament wes tryid,
    That lang befoir in hell wes cryid
        In presens of Mahoun;
    Betuix a telyour and ane sowtar,
    A pricklous and ane hobbell clowttar,   5
        The barres wes maid boun.

The tailyeour, baith with speir and scheild,
Convoyit wes unto the feild
    With mony lymmar loun,
Off seme byttaris and beist knapparis,   10
Of stomok steillaris and clayth takkaris,
    A graceles garisoun.

His baner born wes him befoir,
Quhairin wes clowttis ane hundreth scoir,
    Ilk ane of divers hew;   15
And all stowin out of sindry webbis,
For, quhill the Greik sie flowis and ebbis,
    Telyouris will nevir be trew.
The tailyour on the barres blent;
Allais, he tynt all hardyment,   20
    For feir he chaingit hew:
Mahoun come furth and maid him knycht,
Na ferly thocht his hart wes licht
    That to sic honor grew.

The tailyeour hecht befoir Mahoun   25
That he suld ding the sowtar doun
    Thocht he wer strang as mast;
Bot quhen he on the barres blenkit
The telyouris hairt a littill schrenkit,
    His hairt did all ourcast.   30
Quhen to the sowtar he did cum
Off all sic wirdis he wes full dum,
    So soir he wes agast;
In harte he tuke yit sic ane scunner,
Ane rak of fartis lyk ony thunner   35
    Went fra him, blast for blast.

The sowtar to the feild him drest,
He wes convoyid out of the west
    As ane defender stout:

Suppois he had na lusty varlot,40
He had full mony lowsy harlott
Round rynnand him about.
His baner wes of barkit hyd,
Quhairin Sanct Girnega did glyd
Befoir that rebald rowt;45
Full sowttarlyk he wes of laitis,
For ay betuix the harnes plaitis
The uly birstit out.

Quhen on the telyour he did luke
His hairt a littill dwamyng tuke,50
He mycht nocht rycht upsitt;
In to his stommok wes sic ane steir,
Off all his dennar, quhilk he coft deir,
His breist held deill a bitt.
To comfort him, or he raid forder,55
The Devill off knychtheid gaif him order,
For sair syne he did spitt,
And he about the Devillis nek
Did spew agane ane quart of blek;
Thus knychtly he him quitt.60

Than fourty tymis the Feynd cryd, 'Fy';
The sowtar rycht effeiritly
Unto the feild he socht;
Quhen thay wer servit of thair speiris,
Folk had ane feill be thair effeiris65
Thair hairtis wer baith on flocht.
Thay spurrit thair hors on adir syd,
Syne thay attour the grund cowd glyd,
Than thame togidder brocht;
The tailyeour that wes nocht weill sittin,70
He left his sadill all beschittin
And to the grund he socht.

His harnas brak and maid ane brattill,
The sowtaris hors scart with the rattill
   And round about cowd reill;   75
The beist that frayit wes rycht evill
Ran with the sowtar to the Devill,
   And he rewardit him weill.
Sum thing frome him the Feynd eschewit,
He went agane to bene bespewit,   80
   So stern he wes in steill:
He thocht he wald agane debait him,
He turnd his ers and all bedret him
   Evin quyte from nek till heill.

He lowsit it of with sic a reird,   85
Baith hors and man he straik till eird,
   He fartit with sic ane feir;
'Now haif I quitt the', quod Mahoun;
Thir new maid knychtis lay bayth in swoun
   And did all armes mensweir.   90
The Devill gart thame to dungeoun dryve
And thame of knychtheid cold depryve,
   Dischairgeing thame of weir,
And maid thame harlottis bayth for evir;
Quhilk style to keip thay had fer levir   95
   Nor ony armes beir.

I had mair of thair werkis writtin,
Had nocht the sowtar bene beschittin
   With Belliallis ers unblist;
Bot that sa gud ane bourd me thocht,   100
Sic solace to my hairt it rocht,
   For lawchtir neir I brist;
Quhairthrow I walknit of my trance.
To put this in remembrance
   Mycht no man me resist,   105

For this said justing it befell
Befoir Mahoun the air of hell:
   Now trow this gif ye list.

19

BE TU IX twell houris and ellevin
I dremed ane angell came fra hevin
With plesand stevin sayand on hie,
'Telyouris and sowtaris, blist be ye.

In hevin hie ordand is your place   5
Aboif all sanctis in grit solace,
Nixt God grittest in dignitie:
Tailyouris and sowtaris, blist be ye.

The caus to yow is nocht unkend:
That God mismakkis, ye do amend   10
Be craft and grit agilitie:
Tailyouris and sowtaris, blist be ye.

Sowtaris, with schone weill maid and meit
Ye mend the faltis of ill maid feit,
Quhairfoir to hevin your saulis will fle: 15
Telyouris and sowtaris, blist be ye.

Is nocht in all this fair a flyrok
That hes upoun his feit a wyrok,
Knowll tais, nor mowlis in no degrie,
Bot ye can hyd thame; blist be ye.   20

And ye tailyouris with weill maid clais
Can mend the werst maid man that gais
And mak him semely for to se:
Telyouris and sowtaris, blist be ye.

Thocht God mak ane misfassonit man   25
Ye can him all schaip new agane
And fassoun him bettir be sic thre:
Telyouris and sowtaris, blist be ye.

Thocht a man haif a brokin bak,
Haif he a gude telyour, quhatt rak,   30
That can it cuver with craftis slie:
Telyouris and sowtaris, blist be ye.

Off God grit kyndnes may ye clame,
That helpis his peple fra cruke and lame,
Supportand faltis with your supple: 35
Tailyouris and sowtaris, blist be ye.

In erd ye kyth sic mirakillis heir,
In hevin ye salbe sanctis full cleir,
Thocht ye be knavis in this cuntre:
Telyouris and sowtaris, blist be ye.'   40

MORALITIES

20

HE that hes gold and grit riches
And may be into mirrynes,
And dois glaidnes fra him expell
And levis in to wrechitnes,
He wirkis sorrow to him sell.   5

He that may be but sturt or stryfe
And leif ane lusty plesand lyfe,
And syne with mariege dois him mell
And bindis him with ane wicket wyfe,
He wirkis sorrow to him sell.   10

He that hes for his awin genyie
Ane plesand prop, but mank or menyie,
And schuttis syne at ane uncow schell,
And is forfairn with the fleis of Spenyie,
He wirkis sorrow to him sell.   15

And he that with gud lyfe and trewth,
But varians or uder slewth,
Dois evir mair with ane maister dwell
That nevir of him will haif no rewth,
He wirkis sorrow to him sell.   20

Now all this tyme lat us be mirry
And sett nocht by this warld a chirry,
Now quhill thair is gude wyne to sell:
He that dois on dry breid wirry,
I gif him to the Devill of hell.   25

21

I SE IK about this warld unstabille
To find ane sentence convenabille,
  Bot I can nocht in all my wit
  Sa trew ane sentence fynd off it
As say, it is dessaveabille.   5

For yesterday I did declair
Quhow that the seasoun soft and fair
  Com in als fresche as pako fedder;
  This day it stangis lyk ane edder,
Concluding all in my contrair.   10

Yisterday fair up sprang the flouris,
This day thai ar all slane with schouris;
  And fowllis in forrest that sang cleir
  Now walkis with a drery cheir;
Full caild ar baith thair beddis and bouris.   15

So nixt to summer winter bein,
Nixt efter confort cairis kein,
  Nixt dirk mednycht the mirthefull morrow,
  Nixt efter joy aye cumis sorrow:
So is this warld and ay hes bein.   20

22

  MY heid did yak yester nicht,
This day to mak that I na micht,
  So sair the magryme dois me menyie,
  Perseing my brow as ony ganyie,
That scant I luik may on the licht.   5

And now, schir, laitlie eftir mes
To dyt thocht I begowthe to dres,
  The sentence lay full evill till find;
  Unsleipit in my heid behind,
Dullit in dulnes and distres.   10

Full oft at morrow I upryse,
Quhen that my curage sleipeing lyis;
  For mirth, for menstrallie and play,
  For din nor danceing nor deray,
It will nocht walkin me no wise.   15

23

I THAT in heill wes and gladnes
Am trublit now with gret seiknes
And feblit with infermite:
  Timor mortis conturbat me.

Our plesance heir is all vane glory,   5
This fals warld is bot transitory,
The flesche is brukle, the Fend is sle:
  Timor mortis conturbat me.

The stait of man dois change and vary,
Now sound, now seik, now blith, now sary, 10
Now dansand mery, now like to dee:
  Timor mortis conturbat me.

No stait in erd heir standis sickir;
As with the wynd wavis the wickir,
Wavis this warldis vanite: 15
  Timor mortis conturbat me.

On to the ded gois all estatis,
Princis, prelotis, and potestatis,
Baith riche and pur of al degre:
  Timor mortis conturbat me.   20

He takis the knychtis in to feild,
Anarmit under helme and scheild;
Victour he is at all mellie:
  Timor mortis conturbat me.

That strang unmercifull tyrand 25
Takis, on the moderis breist sowkand,
The bab full of benignite:
   Timor mortis conturbat me.

He takis the campion in the stour,
The capitane closit in the tour, 30
The lady in bour full of bewte:
   Timor mortis conturbat me.

He sparis no lord for his piscence,
Na clerk for his intelligence;
His awfull strak may no man fle: 35
   Timor mortis conturbat me.

Art magicianis and astrologgis,
Rethoris, logicianis and theologgis,
Thame helpis no conclusionis sle:
   Timor mortis conturbat me. 40

In medicyne the most practicianis,
Lechis, surrigianis, and phisicianis,
Thame self fra ded may not supple:
   Timor mortis conturbat me.

I se that makaris amang the laif 45
Playis heir ther pageant, syne gois to graif;
Sparit is nocht ther faculte:
   Timor mortis conturbat me.

He hes done petuously devour
The noble Chaucer of makaris flour, 50
The Monk of Bery, and Gower, all thre:
   Timor mortis conturbat me.

The gude Syr Hew of Eglintoun,
And eik Heryot, and Wyntoun,
He hes tane out of this cuntre: 55
   Timor mortis conturbat me.

That scorpion fell hes done infek
Maister Johne Clerk and James Afflek
Fra ballat making and tragidie:
   Timor mortis conturbat me.   60

Holland and Barbour he hes berevit;
Allace, that he nocht with us levit
Schir Mungo Lokert of the Le:
   Timor mortis conturbat me.

Clerk of Tranent eik he hes tane,   65
That maid the Anteris of Gawane;
Schir Gilbert Hay endit hes he:
   Timor mortis conturbat me.

He hes Blind Hary and Sandy Traill
Slaine with his schour of mortall haill,   70
Quhilk Patrik Johnestoun myght nocht fle:
   Timor mortis conturbat me.

He hes reft Merseir his endite
That did in luf so lifly write,
So schort, so quyk, of sentence hie: 75
   Timor mortis conturbat me.

He hes tane Roull of Aberdene
And gentill Roull of Corstorphin;
Two bettir fallowis did no man se:
   Timor mortis conturbat me.   80

In Dunfermelyne he hes done roune
With Maister Robert Henrisoun.
Schir Johne the Ros enbrast hes he:
   Timor mortis conturbat me.

And he hes now tane last of aw   85
Gud gentill Stobo and Quintyne Schaw,
Of quham all wichtis hes pete:
   Timor mortis conturbat me.

Gud Maister Walter Kennedy
In poynt of dede lyis veraly;   90
Gret reuth it wer that so suld be:
Timor mortis conturbat me.

Sen he hes all my brether tane
He will nocht lat me lif alane;
On forse I man his nyxt pray be: 95
Timor mortis conturbat me.

Sen for the deid remeid is none,
Best is that we for dede dispone
Eftir our deid that lif may we:
Timor mortis conturbat me.   100

24

In to thir dirk and drublie dayis,
Quhone sabill all the hevin arrayis
    With mystie vapouris, cluddis and skyis,
    Nature all curage me denyis
Off sangis, ballattis, and of playis.   5

Quhone that the nycht dois lenthin houris
With wind, with haill and havy schouris,
    My dule spreit dois lurk for schoir;
    My hairt for languor dois forloir
For laik of symmer with his flouris.   10

I walk, I turne, sleip may I nocht,
I vexit am with havie thocht;
    This warld all ouir I cast about,
    And ay the mair I am in dout
The mair that I remeid have socht.   15

I am assayit on everie syde;
Dispair sayis ay,   In tyme provyde,
    And get sum thing quhairon to leif,
    Or with grit trouble and mischeif
Thow sall in to this court abyd.'   20

Than Patience sayis, 'Be not agast,
Hald Hoip and Treuthe within the fast
    And lat Fortoun wirk furthe hir rage,
    Quhome that no rasoun may assuage
Quhill that hir glas be run and past.'   25

And Prudence in my eir sayis ay,
'Quhy wald thow hald that will away
    Or craif that thow may have no space;
    Thow tending to ane uther place,
A journay going everie day?'   30

And than sayis Age, 'My freind, cum neir,
And be not strange, I the requeir;
    Cum brodir, by the hand me tak,
    Remember thow hes compt to mak
Off all thi tyme thow spendit heir.'   35

Syne Deid castis upe his yettis wyd,
Saying, 'Thir oppin sall the abyd;
    Albeid that thow wer never sa stout,
    Undir this lyntall sall thow lowt:
Thair is nane uther way besyde.'   40

For feir of this all day I drowp;
No gold in kist, nor wyne in cowp,
    No ladeis bewtie, nor luiffis blys,
    May lat me to remember this,
How glaid that ever I dyne or sowp.   45

(65)

Yit quhone the nycht begynnis to schort
It dois my spreit sum pairt confort
  Off thocht oppressit with the schowris:
  Cum, lustie symmer, with thi flowris,
That I may leif in sum disport.   50

25

FULL oft I mus and hes in thocht
How this fals warld is ay on flocht,
Quhair no thing ferme is nor degest;
And quhen I haif my mynd all socht,
For to be blyth me think is best.   5

This warld evir dois flicht and vary,
Fortoun sa fast hir quheill dois cary
Na tyme bot turne can it tak rest;
For quhois fals change suld none be sary;
For'to be blyth me thynk it best.   10

Wald man in mynd considdir weill,
Or Fortoun on him turn hir quheill,
That erdly honour may nocht lest,
His fall les panefull he suld feill;
For to be blyth me think it best.   15

Quha with this warld dois warsill and stryfe
And dois his dayis in dolour dryfe,
Thocht he in lordschip be possest
He levis bot ane wrechit lyfe;
For to be blyth me think it best.   20

Off warldis gud and grit riches
Quhat fruct hes man but mirines?
Thocht he this warld had eist and west,
All wer povertie but glaidnes;
For to be blyth me thynk it best.   25

Quho suld for tynsall drowp or de,
For thyng that is bot vanitie,
Sen to the lyfe that evir dois lest
Heir is bot twynklyng of ane e?
For to be blyth me think it best.   30

Had I for warldis unkyndnes
In hairt tane ony havines,
Or fro my plesans bene opprest,
I had bene deid langsyne, dowtles;
For to be blyth me think it best.   35

How evir this warld do change and vary,
Lat us in hairt nevir moir be sary,
Bot evir be reddy and addrest
To pas out of this frawdfull fary;
For to be blyth me think it best.   40

26

QUHAT is this lyfe bot ane straucht way to deid,
    Quhilk hes a tyme to pas and nane to duell;
A slyding quheill us lent to seik remeid,
    A fre chois gevin to paradice or hell,
    A pray to deid, quhome vane is to repell;   5
A schoirt torment for infineit glaidnes,
    Als schort ane joy for lestand hevynes.

27

SALVIOUR, suppois my sensualitie
Subject to syn hes maid my saule of sys,
Sum spark of lycht and spiritualite
Walkynnis my witt, and Ressoun biddis me rys;
My corrupt conscience askis, clips and cryis   5
First grace, syn space for to amend my mys,
Substance with honour, doing none suppryis,
Freyndis, prosperite; heir peax, syne hevynis blys.

28

Now culit is dame Venus brand.
Trew luvis fyre is ay kindilland
And I begyn to undirstand
In feynit luve quhat foly bene;
Now cumis aige quhair yewth hes bene   5
And trew luve rysis fro the splene.

Quhill Venus fyre be deid and cauld
Trew luvis fyre nevir birnis bauld;
So as the ta lufe waxis auld
The tothir dois incres moir kene;   10
Now cumis aige quhair yewth hes bene
And trew lufe rysis fro the splene.

No man hes curege for to wryte
Quhat plesans is in lufe perfyte,
That hes in fenyeit lufe delyt;   15
Thair kyndnes is so contrair clene:
Now cumis aige quhair yewth hes bene
And trew lufe rysis fro the splene.

Full weill is him that may imprent
Or onywayis his hairt consent   20
To turne to trew luve his intent
And still the quarrell to sustene;
Now cumis aige quhair yewth hes bene
And trew lufe rysis fro the splene.

I haif experience by my sell: 25
In luvis court anis did I dwell;
Bot quhair I of a joy cowth tell
I culd of truble tell fyftene;
Now cumis aige quhair yewth hes bene
And trew lufe rysis fro the splene . . .   30

Ane lufe so fare, so gud, so sueit,
So riche, so rewthfull and discreit,
And for the kynd of man so meit,
Nevir moir salbe nor yit hes bene;
Now cumis aige quhair yewth hes bene   35
And trew lufe rysis fro the splene.

Is none sa trew a luve as he
That for trew luve of us did de;
He suld be luffit agane, think me,
That wald sa fane our luve obtene;   40
Now cumis aige quhair yewth hes bene
And trew luve rysis fro the splene.

Is non but grace of God, iwis,
That can in yewth considdir this;
This fals dissavand warldis blis   45
So gydis man in flouris grene;
Now cumis aige quhair yewth hes bene
And trew luve rysis fro the splene.

29

To speik of science, craft, or sapience,
    Off vertew morall, cunnyng, or doctrene,
Off jure, of wisdome, or intelligence,
    Off everie study, lair, or disciplene;
    All is bot tynt or reddie for to tyne,   5
Nocht using it as it sould usit be,
    The craift exerceing, considdering not\the fyne:
A paralous seiknes is vane prosperite.

The curious probatioun logicall,
    The eloquence of ornat rethorie,   10
The naturall science philosophicall,
    The dirk apperance of astronomie,

The theologis sermoun, the fablis of poetrie;
Without gud lyfe all in the selfe dois de
    As Maii flouris dois in September dry: 15
A paralous lyfe is vane prosperite.

Quhairfoir, ye clarkis and grittest of constance,
    Fullest of science and of knawlegeing,
To us be myrrouris in your governance
    And in our darknes be lampis in schyning,   20
    Or than in frustar is your lang leirning;
Giff to your sawis your deidis contrair be,
    Your maist accusar salbe your awin cunning:
A paralus seiknes is vane prosperite.

30

DOVERRIT with dreme, devysing in my slummer
How that this realme with nobillis owt of nummer
Gydit, provydit, sa mony yeiris hes bene,
And now sic hunger, sic cowartis, and sic cummer
Within this land was nevir hard or sene.   5

Sic pryd with prellattis, so few till preiche and pray,
Sic hant of harlettis with thame bayth nicht and day
That sowld haif ay thair God afoir thair ene;
So nyce array, so strange to thair abbay,
Within this land was nevir hard nor sene.   10

So mony preistis cled up in secular weid,
With blasing breistis casting thair clathis on breid—
It is no neid to tell of quhome I mene;
So quhene to reid the deirgey and the beid
Within this land was nevir hard nor sene.   15

So mony maisteris, so mony guckit clerkis,
So mony westaris to God and all his warkis,

So fyry sparkis of dispyt fro the splene,
Sic losin sarkis, so mony glengoir markis,
Within this land was nevir hard nor sene.   20

Sa mony lordis, so mony naturall fulis
That bettir accordis to play thame at the trulis,
Nor seis the dulis that commonis dois sustene;
New tane fra sculis sa mony anis and mulis
Within this land was nevir hard nor sene.   25

Sa mekle tressone, sa mony partiall sawis,
Sa littill ressone to help the commoun cawis,
That all the lawis ar not sett by ane bene;
Sic fenyeit flawis, sa mony waistit wawis,
Within this land was nevir hard nor sene.   30

Sa mony theivis and mycharis weill kend,
Sa grit relevis of lordis thame to defend
Becawis thai spend the pelf thame betwene,
So few till wend this mischeif till amend,
Within this land was nevir hard nor sene.   35

This to correct thay schoir with mony crakkis;
Bot littill effect of speir or battell ax
Quhen curage lakkis, the cors that sowld mak kene;
Sa mony jakkis, and brattis on beggaris bakkis,
Within this land was nevir hard nor sene.   40

Sic vant of vostouris with hairtis in sinfull staturis,
Sic brallaris and bosteris degenerat fra thair naturis,
And sic regratouris the peure men to prevene,
So mony tratouris, sa mony rubeatouris,
Within this land was nevir hard nor sene.   45

Sa mony jugeis and lordis now maid of lait,
Sa small refugeis the peur man to debait,
Sa mony estait, for commoun weill sa quhene,
Ouir all the gait sa mony theivis sa tait,
Within this land was nevir hard nor sene.   50

Sa mony ane sentence retreitit for to win
Geir and acquentance, or kyndnes of thair kyn—
They think no sin quhair proffeit cumis betwene;
Sa mony ane gin to haist thame to the pin
Within this land was nevir hard nor sene.   55

Sic knavis and crakkaris to play at cartis and dyce,
Sic halland schekkaris quhilk at Cowkelbyis gryce
Ar haldin of pryce, quhen lymmaris dois convene;
Sic stoir of vyce, sa mony wittis unwyce,
Within this land was nevir hard nor sene.   60

Sa mony merchandis, sa mony ar mensworne,
Sa peur tennandis, sic cursing evin and morne,
Quhilk slayis the corne and fruct that growis grene;
Sic skaith and scorne, so mony paitlattis worne,
Within this land was nevir hard nor sene.   65

Sa mony rakkettis, sa mony ketchepillaris,
Sic ballis, sic nackettis, and sic tutivillaris,
And sic evill willaris to speik of king and quene,
Sic pudding fillaris discending doun frome millaris,
Within this land was nevir hard nor sene.   70

Sic fartingaillis on flaggis als fatt as quhailis,
Facit lyk fulis with hattis that littill availlis,
And sic fowill tailis, to sweip the calsay clene
The dust upskaillis, sic fillokis with fucksailis,
Within this land was nevir hard nor sene.   75

Sa mony ane kittie drest up with goldin chenye,
So few witty that weill can fabillis fenye,
With apill renye ay schawand hir goldin chene;
Off Sathanis senyie sic ane unsall menyie
Within this land was nevir hard nor sene.   80

31

ANE murlandis man of uplandis mak
At hame thus to his nychtbour spak:
'Quhat tydingis, gossep, peax or weir?'
The tother rownit in his eir,
'I tell yow this undir confessioun;   5
Bot laitly lichtit of my meir,
I come of Edinburch fra the sessioun.'

'Quhat tythingis hard ye thair, I pray yow?'
The tother answerit, 'I sall say yow:
Keip this all secreit, gentill brother;   10
Is na man thair that trestis ane uther;
Ane commoun doar of transgressioun
Of innocent folkis prevenis a futher:
Sic tydingis hard I at the sessioun.

Sum with his fallow rownis him to pleis,   15
That wald for invy byt of his neis;
His fa sum by the oxstar leidis;
Sum patteris with his mowth on beidis
That hes his mynd all on oppressioun;
Sum beckis full law and schawis bair heidis   20
Wald luke full heich, war not the sessioun.

Sum bydand the law layis land in wed,
Sum super expendit gois to his bed;
Sum speidis, for he in court hes menis;
Sum of parcialitie complenis,   25
How feid and favour flemis discretioun;
Sum speiks full fair, and falsly fenis:
Sic tythingis hard I at the sessioun.

Sum castis summondis, and sum exceptis,
Sum standis besyd and skaild law keppis,   30
Sum is continuit, sum wynnis, sum tynis,
Sum makis him mirry at the wynis;

Sum is put owt of his possessioun,
Sum herreit, and on creddens dynis:
Sic tydingis hard I at the sessioun.   35

Sum sweiris and forsaikis God,
Sum in ane lambskin is ane tod,
Sum in his toung his kyndnes tursis,
Sum cuttis throttis, and sum pykis pursis,
Sum gois to gallous with processioun,   40
Sum sanis the sait, and sum thame cursis:
Sic tydingis hard I at the sessioun.

Religious men of divers placis
Cumis thair to wow and se fair facis;
Baith Carmeleitis and Cordilleris   45
Cumis thair to genner and get ma freiris,
And ar unmyndfull of thair professioun;
The yungar at the eldar leiris:
Sic tydingis hard I at the sessioun.

Thair cumis yung monkis of he complexioun,   50
Of devoit mynd, luve, and affectioun,
And in the courte thair hait flesche dantis
Full faderlyk, with pechis and pantis;
Thay ar so humill of intercessioun,
All mercyfull wemen thair eirandis grantis: 55
Sic tydingis hard I at the sessioun.'

32

QUHY will ye marchantis of renoun
Lat Edinburgh your nobill toun
For laik of reformatioun
The commone proffeitt tyine and fame?
     Think ye not schame,   5
That onie uther regioun
Sall with dishonour hurt your name?

May nane pas throw your principall gaittis
For stink of haddockis and of scattis,
For cryis of carlingis and debaittis,   10
For fensum flyttingis of defame:
   Think ye not schame,
Befoir strangeris of all estaittis
That sic dishonour hurt your name?

Your stinkand scull that standis dirk   15
Haldis the lycht fra your parroche kirk,
Your foirstairis makis your housis mirk
Lyk na cuntray bot heir at hame:
   Think ye not schame,
Sa litill polesie to wirk,   20
In hurt and sklander of your name?

At your hie croce quhar gold and silk
Sould be, thair is bot crudis and milk;
And at your trone bot cokill and wilk,
Pansches, pudingis of Jok and Jame: 25
   Think ye not schame,
Sen as the world sayis that ilk
In hurt and sclander of your name?

Your commone menstrallis hes no tone
Bot 'Now the day dawis', and 'Into Joun';   30
Cunningar men man serve Sanct Cloun
And nevir to uther craftis clame:
   Think ye not schame,
To hald sic mowaris on the moyne
In hurt and sclander of your name?   35

Tailyouris, soutteris, and craftis vyll
The fairest of your streitis dois fyll,
And merchandis at the stinkand styll
Ar hamperit in ane hony came:

(75)

Think ye not schame, 40
That ye have nether witt nor wyll
To win yourselff ane bettir name?

Your burgh of beggeris is ane nest,
To schout thai swentyouris will not rest;
All honest folk they do molest, 45
Sa piteuslie thai cry and rame:
    Think ye not schame,
That for the poore hes nothing drest,
In hurt and sclander of your name?

Your proffeit daylie dois incres, 50
Your godlie workis les and les;
Through streittis nane may mak progres
For cry of cruikit, blind and lame:
    Think ye not schame,
That ye sic substance dois posses 55
And will nocht win ane bettir name?

Sen for the court and the sessioun
The great repair of this regioun
Is in your burgh, thairfoir be boun
To mend all faultis that ar to blame, 60
    And eschew schame;
Gif thai pas to ane uther toun
Ye will decay, and your great name.

Thairfoir strangeris and leigis treit,
Tak not ouer meikle for thair meit, 65
And gar your merchandis be discreit.
That na extortiounes be, proclame
    All fraud and schame.
Keip ordour and poore nighbouris beit,
That ye may gett ane bettir name. 70

Singular proffeit so dois yow blind,
The common proffeit gois behind;
I pray that lord remeid to fynd
That deit into Jerusalem,
    And gar you schame;   75
That sum tyme ressoun may yow bind
For to [   ] yow guid name.

33

AIRLIE on As Wodnisday
At the wyne sat cumeris tway:
The tane to the tother cold compleine;
Sichand and soupand can scho say,
'This lange Lentrune hes maid me lene.'   5

Besyd the fyr quhair that scho sat,
God wait gif scho was girt and fat,
Yit to be febill scho did hir fene,
Sayand ay, 'Cumer, lat preif of that;
That Lentrune sall nocht mak us lene.'   10

'Fair gentill cumer', said the tother,
'Ye tak that migarnes of your mother;
Ill wyne to test scho did disdene,
Bot mavessie scho bad nane uther,
That Lentrune suld nocht mak hir lene.   15

Cumer, be blythe bayth evin and morrow
And lat your husband drie the sorrow;
Fra our lang fasting you refrene
And I sall find you, God to borrow,
That Lentrune sall nocht mak you lene.'   20

'Fair gentill cumer,' than said scho,
'All is to tene him that I do;

In bed he is nocht worthe ane bene.
Fill the cop, cumer, and drink me to,
That Lentrune sall nocht mak us lene.'   25

Thir twa out of ane scopin stowp
Tha drank thre quartis, soup and soup,
Sic drouthe and thrist was thame betwene;
Bot thane to mend tha had gud hop
That Lentrune suld nocht mak thame lene.   30

LIFE AT COURT

34

SCHIR JOHINE THE ROS, ane thing thair is compild
  In generale be Kennedy and Quinting,
Quhilk hes thame self aboif the sternis styld;
  Bot had thay maid of mannace ony mynting
  In speciall, sic stryfe sould rys but stynting;   5
Howbeit with bost thair breistis wer als bendit
As Lucifer that fra the hevin discendit,
  Hell sould nocht hyd thair harnis fra harmis hynting.

The erd sould trymbill, the firmament sould schaik,
  And all the air in vennaum suddane stink,   10
And all the divillis of hell for redour quaik
  To heir quhat I sould wryt with pen and ynk:
  For and I flyt, sum sege for schame sould sink,
The se sould birn, the mone sould thoill ecclippis,
Rochis sould ryfe, the warld sould hald no grippis,   15
  Sa loud of cair the commoun bell sould clynk.

Bot wondir laith wer I to be ane baird;
  Flyting to use richt gritly I eschame:
For it is nowthir wynning nor rewaird,
  Bot tinsale baith of honour and of fame,   20
  Incres of sorrow, sklander and evill name.
Yit mycht thay be sa bald in thair bakbytting
To gar me ryme and rais the feynd with flytting,
  And throw all cuntreis and kinrikis thame proclame . . .

Thow speiris, dastard, gif I dar with the fecht: 25
  Ye dagone, dowbart, thairof haif thow no dowt.
Quhair evir we meit thairto my hand I hecht
  To red thy rebald ryming with a rowt;

Throw all Bretane it salbe blawin owt
How that thow, poysonit pelor, gat thy paikis;   30
    With ane doig leich I schepe to gar the schowt
And nowther to the tak knyfe, swerd, nor aix.

Thow crop and rute of traitouris tressonable,
    The fathir and moder of morthour and mischeif,
Dissaitfull tyrand with serpentis tung unstable,   35
    Cuckald cradoun, cowart and commoun theif:
    Thow purpest for to undo our lordis cheif
In Paislay with ane poysone that wes fell;
    For quhilk, brybour, yit sall thow thoill a bɩeif:
Pelour, on the I sall it preif my sell.   40

Thocht I wald lie, thy frawart phisnomy
    Dois manifest thy malice to all men;
Fy, traitour theif; Fy, glengoir loun, fy, fy;
    Fy, feyndly front far fowlar than ane fen.
    My freyindis thow reprovit with thy pen: 45
Thow leis, tratour, quhilk I sall on the preif;
    Suppois thy heid war armit tymis ten
Thow sall recryat, or thy croun sall cleif . . .

Lene larbar, loungeour baith lowsy in lisk and lonye,
    Fy, skolderit skyn, thow art bot skyre and skrumple; 50
For he that rostit Lawarance had thy grunye,
    And he that hid Sanct Johnis ene with ane womple
    And he that dang Sanct Augustine with ane rumple
Thy fowll front had, and he that Bartilmo flaid;
    The gallowis gaipis eftir thy graceles gruntill,   55
As thow wald for ane haggeis, hungry gled.

Commirwald crawdoun, na man comptis the ane kers,
    Sueir swappit swanky, swynekeper ay for swaittis;
Thy commissar Quintyne biddis the cum kis his ers;
    He luvis nocht sic ane forlane loun of laittis: 60

He sayis thow skaffis and beggis mair beir and aitis
Nor ony cripill in Karrik land abowt;
  Uther pure beggaris and thow ar at debaittis;
Decrepit karlingis on Kennedy cryis owt.

Mater annuche I haif, I bid nocht fenyie,   65
  Thocht thow, fowll trumpour, thus upoun me leid;
Corruptit carioun, he sall I cry thy senyie!
  Thinkis thow nocht how thow come in grit neid
  Greitand in Galloway lyk to ane gallow breid,
Ramand and rolpand, beggand koy and ox?   70
  I saw the thair in to thy wathman weid,
Quhilk wes nocht worth ane pair of auld gray sox.

Ersche katherene, with thy polk breik and rilling,
  Thow and thy quene, as gredy gleddis ye gang
With polkis to mylne, and beggis baith meill and schilling; 75
  Thair is bot lys and lang nailis yow amang:
  Fowll heggirbald, for hennis thus will ye hang;
Thow hes ane perrellus face to play with lambis;
  Ane thowsand kiddis, wer thay in faldis full strang,
Thy lymmerfull luke wald fle thame and thair damis.   80

In till ane glen thow hes, owt of repair,
  Ane laithly luge that wes the lippir menis;
With the ane sowtaris wyfe, off blis als bair;
  And lyk twa stalkaris steilis in cokis and hennis;
  Thow plukkis the pultre and scho pullis off the penis.   85
All Karrik cryis, 'God gif this dowsy be drownd!'
  And quhen thow heiris ane guse cry in the glenis
Thow thinkis it swetar than sacrand bell of sound.

Thow Lazarus, thow laithly lene tramort,
  To all the warld thow may example be   90
To luk upoun thy gryslie peteous port;
  For hiddowis, haw and holkit is thyne e,

(81)

Thy cheik bane bair, and blaiknit is thy ble;
Thy choip, thy choll, garris men for to leif chest;
     Thy gane, it garris us think that we mon de: 95
I conjure the, thow hungert heland gaist.

The larbar lukis of thy lang lene craig,
     Thy pure pynit thrott, peilit and owt of ply,
Thy skolderit skin, hewd lyk ane saffrone bag,
     Garris men dispyt thar flesche, thow spreit of Gy;   100
Fy, feyndly front; fy, tykis face, fy, fy:
     Ay loungand lyk ane loikman on ane ledder,
     With hingit luik ay wallowand upone wry
Lyke to ane stark theif glowrand in ane tedder.

Nyse nagus, nipcaik, with thy schulderis narrow,   105
     Thow lukis lowsy, loun of lownis aw;
Hard hurcheoun, hirpland hippit as ane harrow,
     Thy rigbane rattillis, and thy ribbis on raw;
Thy hanchis hirklis with hukebanis harth and haw,
Thy laithly lymis are lene as ony treis: 110
     Obey, theif baird, or I sall brek thy gaw;
Fowll carrybald, cry mercy on thy kneis . . .

Thow held the burcht lang with ane borrowit goun
     And ane caprowsy barkit all with sweit,
And quhen the laidis saw the sa lyk a loun   115
     Thay bickerit the with mony bae and bleit.
     Now upaland thow levis on rubbit quheit;
Oft for ane caus thy burdclaith neidis no spredding,
     For thow hes nowthir for to drink nor eit,
Bot lyk ane berdles baird that had no bedding.   120

Strait Gibbonis air, that nevir ourstred ane hors,
     Bla berfute berne, in bair tyme wes thow borne;
Thow bringis the Carrik clay to Edinburgh Cors
     Upoun thy botingis hobland, hard as horne;

Stra wispis hingis owt quhair that the wattis ar worne: 125
Cum thow agane to skar us with thy strais,
   We sall gar scale our sculis all the to scorne
And stane the up the calsay quhair thow gais.

Off Edinburcht the boyis as beis owt thrawis
   And cryis owt ay, 'Heir cumis our awin queir clerk!' 130
Than fleis thow lyk ane howlat chest with crawis,
   Quhill all the bichis at thy botingis dois bark.
   Than carlingis cryis, 'Keip curches in the merk,
Our gallowis gaipis; lo, quhair ane greceles gais!'
   Ane uthir sayis, 'I se him want ane sark;   135
I reid yow, cummer, tak in your lynning clais.'

Than rynis thow doun the gait with glld of boyis,
   And all the toun tykis hingand in thy heilis;
Of laidis and lownis thair rysis sic ane noyis,
   Quhill runsyis rynnis away with cairt and quheilis 140
   And cager aviris castis bayth coillis and creilis
For rerd of the and rattling of thy butis;
   Fische wyvis cryis fy, and castis doun skillis and skeilis;
Sum claschis the, sum cloddis the on the cutis . . .

Mauch muttoun, byt buttoun, peilit gluttoun, air to
      Hilhous;   145
   Rank beggar, ostir dregar, foule fleggar in the flet;
Chittirlilling, ruch rilling, lik schilling in the milhous;
   Baird rehator, theif of natur, fals tratour, feyindis gett;
   Filling of tauch, rak sauch, cry crauch, thow art oursett;
Muttoun dryver, girnall ryver, yadswyvar, fowll fell the; 150
   Herretyk, lunatyk, purspyk, carlingis pet,
Rottin crok, dirtin dok, cry cok, or I sall quell the.

35
    Sir Jhon Sinclair begowthe to dance
    For he was new cum owt of France;
    For ony thing that he do mycht,

The ane futt yeid ay onrycht
And to the tother wald not gree.   5
Quod ane, 'Tak up the quenis knycht!'
A mirrear dance mycht na man se.

Than cam in Maistir Robert Scha,
He leuket as he culd lern tham a;
Bot ay his ane futt did waver,   10
He stackeret lyk ane strummall aver
That hopschackellt war aboin the kne:
To seik fra Sterling to Stranaver,
A mirrear daunce mycht na man see.

Than cam in the maister almaser,   15
Ane hommiltye jommeltye juffler,
Lyk a stirk stackarand in the ry;
His hippis gaff mony hoddous cry.
John Bute the fule said, 'Waes me,
He is bedirtin, fye, fy!'   20
A mirrear dance mycht na man se.

Than cam in Dunbar the mackar,
On all the flure thair was nane frackar;
And thair he dancet the dirrye dantoun,
He hoppet lyk a pillie wanton   25
For luff of Musgraeffe, men tellis me;
He trippet quhill he tint his panton:
A mirrear dance mycht na man se.

Than cam in Mæsteres Musgraeffe,
Scho mycht heff lernit all the laeffe;   30
Quhen I schau hir sa trimlye dance,
Hir guid convoy and contenance,
Than for hir saek I wissitt to be
The grytast erle or duk in France:
A mirrear dance mycht na man see.   35

Than cam in Dame Dounteboir,
God waett gif that schou louket sowr;
Schou maid sic morgeownis with hir hippis,
For lachtter nain mycht hald thair lippis.

    Quhen schou was danceand bisselye   40
Ane blast of wind son fra hir slippis:
    A mirrear dance mycht na man see.

Quhen thair was cum in fyve or sax
The quenis Dog begowthe to rax;
And of his band he maid a bred,   45
And to the danceing soin him med;
    Quhou mastevlyk about yeid he!
He stinckett lyk a tyk, sum saed:
    A mirrear dance mycht na man se.

36

Now lythis off ane gentill knycht,
Schir Thomas Norny, wys and wycht
    And full off chevelry;
Quhais father was ane giand keyne,
His mother was ane farie queyne,   5
    Gottin be sossery.

Ane fairar knycht nor he was ane,
On ground may nothair ryd nor gane
    Na beire buklar nor brand,
Or com in this court, but dreid;   10
He did full mony valyeant deid
    In Rois and Murray land.

Full many catherein hes he chaist,
And cummerid mony helland gaist
    Amang thay dully glennis;   15
Off the Clen Quhettane twenti scoir
He drave as oxin him befoir,
    This deid thocht na man kennis.

At feastis and brydallis upaland
He wan the gre and the garland,   20
  Dansit non so on deis;
He hes att werslingis bein ane hunder,
Yet lay his body never at under:
  He knawis giff this be leis.

Was never wyld Robein under bewch   25
Nor yet Roger off Clekniskleuch
  So bauld a berne as he;
Gy off Gysburne, na Allan Bell,
Na Simonis sonnes off Quhynfell
  At schot war never so slie.   30

This anterous knycht, quhar ever he went,
At justing and at tornament
  Evermor he wan the gre;
Was never off halff so gryt renowne
Sir Bevis the knycht off Southe Hamptowne,   35
  I schrew him giff I le.

Thairfoir Quenetyne was bot a lurdane
That callit him ane full plum jurdane,
  This wyse and worthie knycht;
He callit him fowlar than a full,   40
He said he was ane licherus bull
  That croynd baith day and nycht.

He wald heff maid him Curris kneff,
I pray God better his honour saiff
  Na to be lychtleit sua;   45
Yet this far furth I dar him prais,
He fyld never sadell in his dais,
  And Curry befyld tua.

Quhairfoir ever at Pesche and Yull
I cry him lord of evere full   50
  That in this regeone duellis;

And verralie that war grit rycht,
For off ane hy renowned knycht
   He wanttis no thing bot bellis.

37

THE Wardraipper of Venus boure,
To giff a doublett he is als doure
As it war off ane futt syd frog:
   Madame, ye heff a dangerous Dog.

Quhen that I schawe to him your markis,   5
He turnis to me again and barkis
As he war wirriand ane hog:
   Madame, ye heff a dangerous Dog.

Quhen that I schawe to him your wrytin
He girnis that I am red for bytin;   10
I wald he had ane havye clog:
   Madame, ye heff ane dangerous Dog.

Quhen that I speik till him freindlyk,
He barkis lyk ane midding tyk
War chassand cattell throu a bog: 15
   Madam, ye heff a dangerous Dog.

He is ane mastive, mekle of mycht
To keip your wardroippe ouer nycht
Fra the grytt Sowdan Gog-ma-gog:
   Madam, ye heff a dangerous Dog.   20

He is owre mekle to be your messan,
Madame, I red you get a less ane;
His gang garris all your chalmeris schog:
   Madam, ye heff a dangerous Dog.

38

O GRACIOUS princes, guid and fair,
Do weill to James your wardraipair,
Quhais faythfull bruder maist freind I am:
    He is na dog, he is a lam.

Thocht I in ballet did with him bourde   5
In malice spack I nevir ane woord,
Bot all, my dame, to do your gam:
    He is na dog, he is a lam.

Your hienes can nocht gett ane meter
To keip your wardrope, nor discreter   10
To rewle your robbis and dres the sam:
    He is na dog, he is a lam.

The wyff that he had in his innis,
That with the taingis wald braek his schinnis,
I wald schou drownet war in a dam: 15
    He is na dog, he is a lam.

The wyff that wald him kuckald mak,
I wald schou war bayth syd and back
Weill batteret with ane barrou tram:
    He is na dog, he is ane lam.   20

He hes sa weill doin me obey
In till all thing, thairfoir I pray
That nevir dolour mak him dram:
    He is na dog, he is a lam.

39

SCHIR, ye have mony servitouris
And officiaris of dyvers curis;
Kirkmen, courtmen, and craftismen fyne,
Doctouris in jure and medicyne,

Divinouris, rethoris, and philosophouris,   5
Astrologis, artistis, and oratouris,
Men of armes and vailyeand knychtis,
And mony uther gudlie wichtis;
Musicianis, menstralis, and mirrie singaris,
Chevalouris, cawandaris, and flingaris,   10
Cunyouris, carvouris, and carpentaris,
Beildaris of barkis and ballingaris,
Masounis lyand upon the land,
And schipwrichtis hewand upone the strand,
Glasing wrichtis, goldsmythis, and lapidaris,   15
Pryntouris, payntouris, and potingaris;
And all of thair craft cunning
And all at anis lawboring,
Quhilk pleisand ar and honorable
And to your hienes profitable,   20
And richt convenient for to be
With your hie regale majestie,
Deserving of your grace most ding
Bayth thank, rewarde, and cherissing.
    And thocht that I amang the laif   25
Unworthy be ane place to have
Or in thair nummer to be tald;
Als lang in mynd my wark sall hald,
Als haill in everie circumstance,
In forme, in mater, and substance,   30
But wering or consumptioun,
Roust, canker or corruptioun,
As ony of thair werkis all,
Suppois that my rewarde be small.
    Bot ye sa gracious ar and meik   35
That on your hienes followis eik
Ane uthir sort, more miserabill,
Thocht thai be nocht sa profitable:
Fenyeouris, fleichouris, and flatteraris,
Cryaris, craikaris, and clatteraris,   40

Soukaris, groukaris, gledaris, gunnaris,
Monsouris of France, gud clarat cunnaris,
Innopportoun askaris of Yrland kynd,
And meit revaris lyk out of mynd,
Scaffaris and scamleris in the nuke,   45
And hall huntaris of draik and duik,
Thrimlaris and thristaris as thay war woid,
Kokenis, and kennis na man of gude,
Schulderaris and schowaris that hes no schame,
And to no cunning that can clame,   50
And can non uthir craft nor curis
Bot to mak thrang, schir, in your duris,
And rusche in quhair thay counsale heir,
And will at na man nurtir leyr:
In quintiscence eik ingynouris joly   55
That far can multiplie in folie,
Fantastik fulis bayth fals and gredy,
Off toung untrew and hand evill diedie:
Few dar of all this last additioun
Cum in tolbuyth without remissioun.   60

    And thocht this nobill cunning sort
Quhom of befoir I did report
Rewardit be, it war bot ressoun,
Thairat suld no man mak enchessoun;
Bot quhen the uther fulis nyce   65
That feistit at Cokelbeis gryce
Ar all rewardit, and nocht I,
Than on this fals world I cry, fy:
My hart neir bristis than for teyne,
Quhilk may nocht suffer nor sustene   70
So grit abusioun for to se
Daylie in court befoir myn e.
    And yit more panence wald I have,
Had I rewarde amang the laif:
It wald me sumthing satisfie   75
And les of my malancolie,

And gar me mony falt ouerse
That now is brayd befoir myn e:
My mind so fer is set to flyt
That of nocht ellis I can endyt, 80
For owther man my hart to breik
Or with my pen I man me wreik;
And sen the tane most nedis be,
In to malancolie to de
Or lat the vennim ische all out, 85
Be war, anone, for it will spout,
Gif that the tryackill cum nocht tyt
To swage the swalme of my despyt.

40

SCHIR, for your grace bayth nicht and day
Richt hartlie on my kneis I pray
With all devotioun that I can,
God gif ye war Johne Thomsounis man.

For war it so, than weill war me, 5
But benefice I wald nocht be;
My hard fortoun wer endit than:
God gif ye war Johne Thomsounis man.

Than wald sum reuth within yow rest
For saik of hir, fairest and best 10
In Bartane, sen hir tyme began:
God gif ye war Johne Thomsounis man.

For it micht hurt in no degre
That one so fair and gude as sche
Throw hir vertew sic wirschip wan 15
Als yow to mak Johne Thomsounis man.

I wald gif all that ever I have
To that conditioun, sa God me saif,

That ye had vowit to the swan
   Ane yeir to be Johne Thomsounis man.   20

The mersy of that sweit meik Rois
Suld soft yow, Thirsill, I suppois,
Quhois pykis throw me so reuthles ran:
   God gif ye war Johne Thomsounis man.

My advocat bayth fair and sweit,   25
The hale rejosing of my spreit,
Wald speid in to my erand than:
   And ye war anis Johne Thomsounis man.

Ever quhen I think yow harde or dour
Or mercyles in my succour,   30
Than pray I God and sweit Sanct An,
   Gif that ye war Johne Thomsounis man.

41

SCHIR, yit remembir as of befoir
How that my yowth is done forloir
In your service, with pane and greif;
Gud consciens cryis reward thairfoir:
   Exces of thocht dois me mischeif. . . .   5

In sum parte on my self I plenye,
Quhen udir folkis dois flattir and fenye;
Allace, I can bot ballattis breif,
Sic bairneheid biddis my brydill renye:
   Exces of thocht dois me mischeif.   10

I grant my service is bot licht;
Thairfoir of mercy and nocht of richt
I ask you, schir, no man to greif,
Sum medecyne gife that ye mycht:
   Exces of thocht dois me mischeif.   15

May nane remeid my melady
Sa weill as ye, schir, veraly;
For with a benefice ye may preif,
And gif I mend nocht hestely,
Exces of thocht lat me mischeif.   20

I wes in yowth on nureis kne
Cald, 'dandely, bischop, dandely';
And quhen that age now dois me greif
Ane semple vicar I can nocht be:
Exces of thocht dois me mischeif.   25

Jok that wes wont to keip the stirkis
Can now draw him ane cleik of kirkis,
With ane fals cairt in to his sleif
Worth all my ballattis undir the birkis:
Exces of thocht dois me mischeif.   30

Twa curis or thre hes upolandis Michell,
With dispensationis bund in a knitchell,
Thocht he fra nolt had new tane leif;
He playis with totum and I with nichell:
Exces of thocht dois me mischeif.   35

How suld I leif that is nocht landit,
Nor yit with benefice am I blandit:
I say nocht, schir, yow to repreif,
Bot doutles I ga rycht neir hand it:
Exces of thocht dois me mischeif.   40

As saul is heir in purgatory
Leving in pane and houp of glory,
Seand my self I haif beleif,
In houp, schir, of your adjutory:
Exces of thocht dois me mischeif.   45

42

SCHIR, lett it nevir in toun be tald
  That I suld be ane Yuillis yald.

Suppois I war ane ald yaid aver
Schott furth our clewch to squische the clever,
And hed the strenthis off all Strenever,   5
I wald at Youll be housit and stald.
  Schir, lat it never in toune be tald
  That I suld be ane Yuillis yald.

I am ane auld hors, as ye knaw,
That ever in duill dois drug and draw;   10
Great court hors puttis me fra the staw
To fang the fog be firthe and fald.
  Schir, lat it never in toune be tald
  That I suld be ane Yuillis yald.

I heff run lang furth in the feild   15
On pastouris that ar plane and peld;
I mycht be now tein in for eild,
My bekis ar spruning he and bald.
  Schir, lat it never in toun be tald
  That I suld be ane Yuillis yald.   20

My maine is turned in to quhyt,
And thair off ye heff all the wyt:
Quhen uthair hors hed brane to byt
I gat bot gris, grype giff I wald.
  Schir, lat it never in towne be tald   25
  That I suld be ane Yuillis yald.

I was never dautit in to stabell,
My lyff hes bein so miserabell,
My hyd to offer I am abell
For evill schoud strae that I reiv wald.   30
  Schir, lat it never in towne be tald
  That I suld be ane Yuillis yald.

And yett suppois my thrift be thyne,
Gif that I die your aucht within,
Lat nevir the soutteris have my skin,   35
With uglie gumes to be knawin.
    Schir, lat it nevir in toun be tald
    That I suld be ane Yuillis yald.

The court hes done my curage cuill
And maid me ane forriddin muill;   40
Yett, to weir trapperis at the Yuill,
I wald be spurrit at everie spald.
    Schir, lat it nevir in toun be tald
    That I suld be ane Yuillis yald.

Now lufferis cummis with larges lowd;   45
Quhy sould not palfrayis thane be prowd
Quhen gillettis wil be schomd and schroud,
That ridden ar baith with lord and lawd?
    Schir, lat it nevir in toun be tald
    That I suld be ane Youllis yald.   50

Quhen I was young and into ply
And wald cast gammaldis to the sky,
I had beine bocht in realmes by
Had I consentit to be sauld.
    Schir, lett it nevir in toun be tauld   55
    That I suld be ane Youllis yald.

With gentill hors quhen I wald knyp,
Thane is thair laid on me ane quhip;
To colleveris than man I skip,
That scabbit ar, hes cruik and cald.   60
    Schir, lett it nevir in toun be tald
    That I suld be ane Youllis yald.

Thocht in the stall I be not clappit
As cursouris that in silk beine trappit,
With ane new hous I wald be happit   65

Aganis this Crysthinmes for the cald.
  Schir, lett it nevir in toun be tald
  That I suld be ane Yuillis yald.

Respontio Regis

Efter our wrettingis, thesaurer,
Tak in this gray hors, auld Dumbar, 70
Quhilk in my aucht with service trew
In lyart changeit is in hew:
Gar hows him now aganis this Yuill
And busk him lyk ane bischopis muill,
For with me hand I have indost 75
To pay quhatevir his trappouris cost.

43

I, MAISTER ANDRO KENNEDY,
  Curro quando sum vocatus,
Gottin with sum incuby
  Or with sum freir infatuatus;
In faith I can nought tell redly 5
  Unde aut ubi fui natus,
Bot in treuth I trow trewly
  Quod sum dyabolus incarnatus.

Cum nichill sit certius morte,
  We mon all de quhen we haif done, 10
Nescimus quando vel qua sorte,
  Na blind Allane wait of the mone,
Ego pacior in pectore,
  This night I mycht nocht sleip a wink;
Licet eger in corpore 15
  Yit wald my mouth be wet with drink.

Nunc condo testamentum meum,
  I leiff my saull for evermare

Per omnipotentem deum
   In to my lordis wyne cellar;   20
Semper ibi ad remanendum
   Quhill domisday without dissever,
Bonum vinum ad bibendum
   With sueit Cuthbert that luffit me nevir . . .

A barell bung ay at my bosum,   25
   Of warldis gud I bad na mair;
Corpus meum ebriosum
   I leif on to the toune of Air;
In a draf mydding for ever and ay
   Ut ibi sepeliri queam,   30
Quhar drink and draff may ilka day
   Be cassyne super faciem meam . . .

To Master Johne Clerk syne
   Do et lego intime
Goddis malisone and myne,   35
   Ipse est causa mortis mee:
War I a dog and he a swyne
   Multi mirantur super me,
Bot I suld ger that lurdane quhryne
   Scribendo dentes sine de.   40

Residuum omnium bonorum
   For to dispone my lord sall haif,
Cum tutela puerorum
   Ade, Kytte, and all the laif.
In faith I will na langar raif: 45
   Pro sepultura ordino
On the new gys, sa God me saif,
   Non sicut more solito.

In die mee sepulture
   I will nane haif bot our awne gyng,   50
Et duos rusticos de rure
   Berand a barell on a styng:

Drynkand and playand cop out, evin
    Sicut egomet solebam;
Singand and gretand with hie stevin,   55
    Potum meum cum fletu miscebam.

I will na preistis for me sing
    Dies illa, dies ire,
Na yit na bellis for me ring
    Sicut semper solet fieri: 60
Bot a bag pipe to play a spryng,
    Et unum ail wosp ante me;
In stayd of baneris for to bring
    Quatuor lagenas cervisie,
Within the graif to set sic thing   65
    In modum crucis juxta me,
To fle the fendis, than hardely sing
    De terra plasmasti me.

44

WE that ar heir in hevins glory
To yow that ar in purgatory
Commendis us on our hairtly wyis;
I mene we folk in parradyis
In Edinburcht, with all mirrines,   5
To yow of Strivilling in distres,
Quhair nowdir plesance nor delyt is;
For pety this epistell wrytis.
O ye heremeitis and hankersaidilis
That takis your pennance at your tablis,   10
And eitis nocht meit restorative,
Nor drynkis no wyn confortative,
Bot aill, and that is thyn and small,
With few coursis into your hall;
But cumpany of lordis and knychtis   15
Or ony uder gudly wichtis,

Solitar walkand your allone,
Seing no thing bot stok and stone;
Out of your panefull purgatory
To bring yow to the blis and glory   20
Off Edinburgh, the mirry toun,
We sall begyn ane cairfull soun,
Ane dergy devoit and meik,
The Lord of blis doing beseik
Yow to delyver out of your noy   25
And bring yow sone to Edinburgh joy,
For to be mirry amang us;
And sa the dergy begynis thus:

Lectio prima.

The Fader, the Sone, and Haly Gaist,
The mirthful Mary, virgene chaist,   30
Of angellis all the ordouris nyne,
And all the hevinly court devyne,
Sone bring yow fra the pyne and wo
Of Strivilling, every court manis fo,
Agane to Edinburghis joy and blis,   35
Quhair wirschep, welth, and weilfar is,
Pley, plesance, and eik honesty:
Say ye amen for cherite.

Responsio, Tu autem Domine.

Tak consolatioun   In your pane,
In tribulatioun   Tak consolatioun,   40
Out of vexatioun   Cum hame agane,
Tak consolatioun   In your pane.

Jube Domine benedicere.

Oute of distres of Strivilling toun
To Edinburcht blis God mak yow boun.

(99)   I

Lectio secunda.

Patriarchis, profeitis, and appostillis deir,   45
Confessouris, virgynis, and marteris cleir,
And all the saitt celestiall;
Devotely we upoun thame call,
That sone out of your panis fell
Ye may in hevin heir with us dwell,   50
To eit swan, cran, pertrik, and plever,
And every fische that swymis in rever;
To drynk with us the new fresche wyne
That grew upoun the rever of Ryne,
Fresche fragrant clairettis out of France,   55
Of Angers and of Orliance,
With mony ane cours of grit dyntie:
Say ye amen for cheritie. . . .

Responsorium.

Cum hame and dwell   No moir in Strivilling,
Frome hiddous hell   Cum hame and dwell,   60
Quhair fische to sell   Is non bot spirling;
Cum hame and dwell   No moir in Strivilling.
Et ne nos inducas in temptationem de Strivilling:
Sed libera nos a malo illius.
Requiem Edinburgi dona eis, Domine,   65
Et lux ipsius luceat eis.
A porta tristitie de Strivilling,
Erue, Domine, animas et corpora eorum.
Credo gustare statim vinum Edinburgi,
In villa viventium: 70
Requiescant Edinburgi. Amen.
Deus qui iustos et corde humiles
Ex omni eorum tribulatione liberare dignatus es,
Libera famulos tuos apud villam de Stirling versantes
A penis et tristitiis eiusdem,   75
Et ad Edinburgi gaudia eos perducas,
Ut requiescat Strivilling. Amen.

45

My gudame wes a gay wif, bot scho wes ryght gend;
  Scho duelt furth fer in to France apon Falkland Fell:
Thay callit her Kynd Kittok, quhasa hir weill kend:
  Scho wes like a caldrone cruke, cler under kell;
Thay threpit that scho deit of thirst and maid a gud end. 5
  Efter hir dede scho dredit nought in hevin for to duell,
And sa to hevin the hieway dreidles scho wend,
    Yit scho wanderit and yeid by to ane elriche well.
      Scho met thar, as I wene,
        Ane ask rydand on a snaill,   10
        And cryit, 'Ourtane, fallow, haill!'
        And raid ane inche behind the taill
    Till it wes neir evin.

Sa scho had hap to be horsit to hir herbry
  Att ane ailhous neir hevin, it nyghttit thaim thare;   15
Scho deit of thrist in this warld, that gert hir be so dry,
  Scho never eit, bot drank our mesur and mair.
Scho slepit quhill the morne at none and rais airly,
  And to the yettis of hevin fast can the wif fair,
And by Sanct Petir in at the yet scho stall prevely: 20
  God lukit and saw hir lattin in, and lewch his hert sair.
    And thar yeris sevin
      Scho levit a gud life,
      And wes our Ladyis hen wif,
      And held Sanct Petir at strif   25
    Ay quhill scho wes in hevin.

Sche lukit out on a day and thoght ryght lang
  To se the ailhous beside, in till ane evill hour;
And out of hevin the hie gait cought the wif gaing
  For to get hir ane fresche drink; the aill of hevin was
        sour.   30

Scho come againe to hevinnis yet quhen the bell rang;
   Saint Petir hat hir with a club, quhill a gret clour
Rais in hir heid, becaus the wif yeid wrang.
   Than to the ailhous agane scho ran the pycharis to pour,
      And for to brew and baik.   35
         Frendis, I pray yow hertfully,
         Gif ye be thristy or dry
         Drink with my guddame, as ye ga by,
   Anys, for my saik.

46

     HARRY, harry, hobbillschowe:
     Se quha is cummyn nowe,
     Bot I wait nevir howe,
        With the quhorle wynd:
     A soldane owt of Seriand land,   5
     A gyand strang for to stand,
     That with the strenth of my hand
        Beres may bynd.
     Yit I trowe that I vary;
     I am the nakit blynd Hary,   10
     That lang has bene in the fary
        Farleis to fynd;
     And yit gif this be nocht I,
     I wait I am the spreit of Gy,
     Or ellis go by the sky,   15
        Licht as the lynd.

     The God of most magnificence
     Conserf this fair presens,
     And saif this amyable audiens,
        Grete of renoune: 20
     Provest, baillies, officeris,
     And honorable induellaris,
     Marchandis and familiaris
        Of all this fair towne:

Quha is cummyn heir bot I,   25
A bauld, bustuos bellamy,
At your cors to mak a cry
    With a hie sowne?
Quhilk generit am of gyandis kynd
Fra strang Hercules by strynd;   30
Off all the Occident of Ynd
    My eldaris bair the croune.

My foregrantschir hecht Fyn McKowle
That dang the devill and gart him yowle;
The skyis ranyd quhen he wald scowle   35
    And trublit all the aire:
He gat my grantschir Gog Magog,
Ay quhen he dansit the warld wald schog;
Five thousand ellis yeid in his frog
    Of hieland pladdis of haire.   40
Yit he was bot of tender youth;
Bot eftir he grewe mekle at fouth,
Ellevyne ell wyde met was his mouth,
    His teith was tene myle sqwaire.
He wald apone his tais stand   45
And tak the sternis doune with his hand,
And set tham in a gold garland
    Abone his wyfis haire.

He had a wyf was lang of clift,
Hir heid wan heiar than the lift;   50
The hevyne rerdit quhen scho wald rift,
    The las was no thing sklender:
Scho spittit Lochlomond with hir lippis,
Thunner and fyreflaucht flew fra hir hippis,
Quhen scho was crabit the son tholit clips; 55
    The fende durst nocht offend hir.
For cald scho tuke the fever cartane;
For all the claith of Fraunce and Bertane

(103)

Wald nocht be till hir leg a gartane,
   Thocht scho was ying and tender;   60
Apon a nycht heire in the north
Scho tuke the gravell and stalit Cragorth,
Scho pischit the mekle watter of Forth,
   Sic tyde ran eftirhend hir.
A thing writtin of hir I fynd: 65
In Irland quhen scho blewe behynd,
At Noroway costis scho rasit the wynd,
   And gret schippis drownit thare:
Scho fischit all the Spanye seis
With hir sark lape befor hir theis;   70
Sevyne dayis saling betuix hir kneis
   Was estymit, and maire.
The hyngand brayis on athir syde
Scho poltit with hir lymmis wyde;
Lassis mycht leir at hir to stryd   75
   Wald ga to lufis laire.
Scho merkit syne to land with myrth;
And pischit fyf quhalis in the firth
That cropyn war in hir count for girth,
   Welterand amang the waire.   80

My fader, mekle Gow Makmorne,
Out of that wyfis wame was schorne;
For litilnes scho was forlorne
   Sic a kempe to beire.
Or he of eld was yeris thre   85
He wald step oure the occeane se;
The mone sprang never abone his kne,
   The hevyn had of him feire.
Ane thousand yere is past fra mynd
Sen I was generit of his kynd,   90
Full far amang the desertis of Ynde
   Amang lyoun and beire:
Baith the King Arthour and Gawane,

And mony bald berne in Brettane,
Ar deid and in the weiris slane   95
   Sen I couth weild a speire.

I have bene forthwart ever in feild,
And now so lang I haf born scheld
That I am all crynd in for eild
   This litill, as ye may se: 100
I have bene bannist under the lynd
Full lang, that no man couth me fynd,
And now with this last southin wynd
   I am cummyn heir, parde.
My name is Welth, thairfor be blyth;   105
I come heire comfort yow to kyth:
Suppos that wretchis wryng and wryth,
   All darth I sall gar de.
For sekerly, the treuth to tell,
I come amang yow heire to duell;   110
Fra sound of Sanct Gelis bell
   Nevir think I to fle.

Sophea and the Soldane strang
With weiris that has lestit lang
Furth of thar boundis maid me to gang,   115
   And turn to Turky tyte:
The King of Frauncis gret army
Has brocht in darth in Lombardy,
And in ane cuntre he and I
   May nocht baith stand perfyte.   120
In Denmark, Swetherik, and Noroway,
Na in the[r] steidis I dar nocht ga,
Amang thaim is bot tak and sla,
   Cut thropillis and mak quyte.
Irland for evir I have refusit,   125
All wichtis suld hald me excusit,
For never in land quhar Erische was usit
   To duell had I delyte.

Quharfor in Scotland come I heire,
With yow to byde and perseveire 130
In Edinburgh, quhar is meriast cheire,
  Plesans, disport, and play;
Quhilk is the lampe and A per se
Of this regioun in all degre,
Of welefaire and of honeste, 135
  Renoune, and riche aray.
Sen I am Welth cummyn to this wane,
Ye noble merchandis everilkane
Addres yow furth with bow and flane
  In lusty grene lufraye; 140
And follow furth on Robyn Hude
With hartis coragious and gud,
And, thocht that wretchis wald ga wod,
  Of worschipe hald the way.

For I and my thre feres aye, 145
Weilfaire, Wantones, and Play,
Sall byde with yow in all affray,
  And cair put clene to flicht;
And we sall dredles us addres
To bannis derth and all distres, 150
And with all sportis and merynes
  Your hartis hald ever on hicht.
I am of mekle quantite,
Of gyand kynd, as ye may se;
Quhar sall be gottin a wyf to me 155
  Siclyke of breid and hicht?
I dreid that thair be nocht a maide
In all this towne may me abyd;
Quha wait gif ony heir besyd
  Micht suffir me all nycht? 160

With yow sen I mon leid my lyf,
Gar sers baith Louthiane and Fyf

And wale to me a mekle wyf,
  A gret ungracious gan,
Sen scho is gane, the gret forlore . . .   165

Adow, fair weill, for now I go,
Bot I will nocht lang byd yow fro;
Chryst yow conserve fra every wo,
  Baith madin, wyf, and man;
God bliss thame, and the haly rude.   170
Givis me a drink, sa it be gude,
And quha trowis best that I do lude
  Skynk first to me the can.

NOTES

1. *Rorate celi desuper*

1, 8. The Latin phrases, from the services for Christmas Eve and Christmas Day, are derived from Isa. xlv. 8 and ix. 6.

3–7. *now is rissin the bricht day ster*, &c. See Rev. xxii. 16.

9–10. *Archangellis . . . potestatis*: orders of the hierarchies of heaven, elaborated in the Middle Ages from Col. i. 16 and similar texts. The first hierarchy comprises seraphim, cherubim, and thrones; the second, dominations, virtues, and powers; and the third, principalities, archangels, and angels.

43. *the blissit frute*. Cf. the *Ave Maria*, 'benedicta tu in mulieribus, et benedictus fructus ventris tui'.

49. *hevin imperiall* (*coelum empyreum*), the highest heaven and the dwelling of God and his angels.

2. *Amang thir freiris within ane cloister*

With Dunbar's account of the Passion, and his introduction of abstract virtues, compare Langland, *Piers Plowman*, B. xviii, and Walter Kennedy's *Passioun* (*Devotional Pieces*, ed. Bennett, S.T.S., 1955, pp. 7 ff.; v. ibid. p. 226 for another text of Dunbar's poem).

7. **gaude flore [virginali],** the opening of a hymn to the Virgin.

3. *Done is a battell on the dragon blak*

For more elaborate descriptions of the harrowing of hell, see *Piers Plowman*, B. xviii and xix, and the York *Harrowing* (*Fourteenth Century Verse and Prose*, ed. Sisam, XVI).

8. **Surrexit dominus**, the first versicle for matins on Easter Sunday.

10. *the crewall serpent with the mortall stang*. See Gen. iii. 15.

19. *lyk a lyone*. In the Bestiaries the lion cub is brought to life by the breath of its father on the third day—a type of the Resurrection.

20. *as a gyane*, breaking the gates of hell as his antitype Samson bore off the gates of Gaza; cf. Langland, *Piers Plowman*, B. xviii. 258–9.

22. Christ the sun of righteousness (Mal. iv. 2) is identified with Apollo, god of the sun.

27. *The sone that wox all paill.* Cf. 2. 84–85.

29. *The knell of mercy.* An allusion to the ringing of bells on Easter Sunday. Cf. *Piers Plowman*, B. xviii. 425.

4. *Hale, sterne superne, hale in eterne*

In metre and internal rhyme, imagery, and diction, modelled on Latin hymns to the Virgin. An extreme example of 'aureation'. Cf. Henryson, *Ane Prayer for the Pest*, sts. 9–11.

5. *Quhen Merche wes with variant windis past*

Included by Allan Ramsay in *The Ever Green* (1724) with the title 'The Thistle and the Rose'. The marriage of James IV and Margaret Tudor, celebrated in this poem, took place at Edinburgh on 8 August 1503. For a contemporary account see Agnes Mure Mackenzie, *Scottish Pageant*, i (1952), 110–22.

In the setting of his dream and the description of Nature's parliament Dunbar owes much to the example of Chaucer's *Parlement of Foules*, and he adopts Chaucer's stanza. For other gatherings of animals in early Scottish poetry see *The Kingis Quair*, sts. 152–8, and Henryson, *Fabillis*, sts. 121 ff. The climax of the poem is Nature's injunction to the rulers of the beasts, birds, and plants—King James in three heraldic representations—and the celebration of the Rose. The thistle and the rose were already associated as emblems of the marriage: the new windows of Holyrood Palace carried the arms of Scotland and England with a thistle and a rose interlaced through a crown, and James's marriage contract was bordered in intertwined roses, thistles, and marguerites. Cf. 40. 21–24.

37. *Uprys*, &c. Cf. Chaucer, *C.T.*, A. 1041–5.

46. *eftir hir*: supplied by Allan Ramsay. The MS. repeats 'full haistely' from the preceding line.

49. *levis . . . fleit*: 'leaves wet with the dew flowing down'.

83. *yarrow*, milfoil: used by witches to give them swiftness in night rides (S.T.S. edn.).

92. *This awfull beist*: the emblem of royal mercy, and the royal arms of Scotland, described in *The Buke of the Howlat* (see 23. 61–63, note), as a lion

> Maid maikles of mycht, on mold quhair he movit
> Rycht rampand as roy ryell of array.

Off pure gold wes the grund, quhair the grym hovit,
With dowble tressour about, flowrit in fay;
And flourdelycis on loft, that mony leid lovit;
Of gold signet and set, to schaw in assay. . . .[1]

119. **parcere prostratis**: part of a motto associated with the armorial bearings of the Scottish kings and derived from Pliny's 'leoni tantum ex feris clementia in supplices; prostratis parcit' (*Nat. Hist.* viii. 19).

120. *the Egle*, the emblem of royal liberality. 'The prey that she taketh, but it be for great hunger, she eateth not alone but putteth it forth in common to fowls that follow her' (Bartholomeus Anglicus, *De Proprietatibus Rerum*).

142. *reid and quhyt*: a stock phrase (cf. 11. 12), here peculiarly appropriate to the daughter of Elizabeth of York and the Lancastrian Henry VII.

143. *honesty*, reputation.   150. *the lilly*, France.

153. *Cum, blowme of joy*, &c. An application of the verse *Veni, coronaberis* (Song of Songs, iv. 8).

167. An adaptation of the Nativity symbol, Mary giving birth to the fleur-de-lis. Cf. *Early English Lyrics*, ed. Chambers and Sidgwick, 1907, No. lxxv.

6. *Blyth Aberdeane, thow beriall of all tounis*

In 1580 the Provost of Aberdeen reminded the Council of the 'lovabill consuetud of this realme obseruit perpetuallie in all tyme bigane' by the Scottish boroughs, in receiving royalty 'with willing and glaid hartis schawing significatioun thairof at thair vtermaist power to recreat and glaid the kyngis maiestie with farceis, playis, historeis, antikis and . . . vther decoratioun' (A. J. Mill, *Medieval Plays in Scotland*, 1927, p. 161). Queen Margaret entered Aberdeen in May 1511. The borough set itself to receive her 'als honorablie as ony burgh of Scotland except Edinburgh allanerlie'; the streets were cleaned 'of all myddingis', and the citizens were ordered to 'furnys and graith the staris' outside their houses 'with arres werk daily' (ibid., p. 158). Dunbar's poem is the only record of the pageants

---

[1] *Maikles*, matchless; *mold*, earth; *grym*, fierce one; *hovit*, hung; *tressour*, border; *in fay*, rightly; *leid*, people; *signet and set*, devised and mounted; *assay*, battle.

(representing the *Salutation, Magi, Expulsion from Eden*, &c.)
provided in Margaret's honour. Similar entertainments are
described in Mill, op. cit., pp. 78–85.

42. *claid in greine*. The costume in which maidens did honour
to May. Cf. 11. 60; Chaucer, *C.T.*, A. 1686.

47. *saluand*. The MS. has 'husband'; but a king's presence is
not so incidentally noted.

7. *Renownit, ryall, right reverend and serene*

The Chepman and Myllar Print is headed: 'The ballade of ane
right noble victorius and myghty lord Barnard Stewart lord of
Aubigny erle of Beaumont . . . consaloure and chamerlane
ordinare to the maist hee maist excellent and maist crystyn
prince Loys king of france knyght of his ordoure Capitane of
the kepyng of his body Conquereur of Naplis and umquhile
constable general of the same Compilit be Maistir Willyam
dumbar at the said lordis cumyng to Edinburghe in Scotland
send in ane ryght excellent embassat. . . .' Aubigny arrived on
9 May 1508; 'and the kingis grace treittit him verie weill and
gentellie, and sett him ever at the tabill with him self and maid
him iudge in all his iusting and tornamentis, callit him father of
weir because he was practissit in the samin' (Pitscottie, *Historie*,
S.T.S., i. 241–2). Cf. 8, introd. note. The present poem was
doubtless planned as part of the official reception. The Stewarts
were one of several Scottish families who in the fifteenth century
served the kings of France. Aubigny died a few weeks later,
and Dunbar lamented his death in an elegy.

33. *Mars . . . armipotent*. Cf. Virgil, *Aen*. ix. 717, 'Mars
armipotens'; Chaucer, *C.T.*, A. 1982 (translating Boccaccio's
'armipotente').

35. *Saturnus*: usually baleful in his effects: cf. *C.T.*, A. 2453 ff.,
and 16. 31.

38. *Marcurius*, Mercury, god of eloquence. Cf. Henryson,
Testament, st. 35.

39. *Fortuna Maior*. The name of a figure of the stars in geo-
mancy: cf. *Purgatorio*, xix. 4–6, and *Troilus and Criseyde*, iii. 1420.

44–45. *quhat feildis thou wan*, &c. Aubigny led the French
auxiliaries at Bosworth (1485) in support of Henry Tudor, fought
against Cordova in Italy in 1495 and gained Naples, and defeated
a Spanish army again in Calabria in 1503.

8. *Lang heff I maed of ladyes quhytt*

'Quod dunbar of an blak moir' (Maitland). By his encourage-
ment of feats of arms James 'brocht his realme to great man-
heid and honouris . . . quhilk caussit mony forand knychtis to
come out of strange contrieis to Scotland to seik iusting'
(Pitscottie, i. 232). The occasion of this poem was a tournament
initiated by a French visitor, the Sieur de la Bastie, in 1507,
and repeated in the presence of Aubigny (see 7, introd. note) in
1508. 'Thair come ane knycht and ane lady callit the quhyt
rois; [thaireftir] the king gart set the haill justing and callit the
samin the turnament of the black knicht and the black lady'—
probably one of the 'Moris [Negro] lasses' of the court records.
'This turnament and iusting beand indureit the space of xl
dayis . . . the king causit to mak ane gret triumphe and bancat
in Halyrudhous quhilk lestit the space of thrie dayis' (Pitscottie,
i. 242–4). Dunbar's response to these elaborate ceremonies,
starting from the original contrast between the 'quyht rois' and
the 'blak moir', is characteristically novel and ribald.

11. *claid in reche apparrall.* The lady sat in a 'chair trium-
phale' adorned with red taffeta; she wore a gown of gold-
flowered damask, with bordering in green and yellow taffeta,
and black sleeves and gloves; and her attendants were dressed
in white coats and green and yellow taffeta gowns (*Accounts of
the Lord High Treasurer of Scotland*, 1507).

10. *Sen that I am a presoneir*

The stock metaphor of a lover held in thrall to his mistress's
beauty is expanded into a concise allegory of courtship and
marriage, perhaps after the design of a court pageant. The ulti-
mate source of the allegory is the psychological drama in the
Roman de la Rose, describing a lover's vision of his attempt to
possess his lady's love (symbolized by the Rose): he is aided by
Franchise, Pity, and Belacueil (Fair Welcome), symbols of her
generosity and her readiness to accept his love, and opposed by
Danger, Chastity, Fear, and Slander, symbols of her defensive
reticence and her dread of dishonour. Dunbar modifies the
formula. The lover is imprisoned by the lady's beauty and
secured by her reticence and indifference; he counter-attacks
with the conventional auxiliaries and gains her love; and the

consequent assaults of Slander and Envy are repelled by Matrimony—an extension of the traditional campaign in *amour courtois*, which ends with possession.

5. *I govit on that gudliest.* In the psychology of love, violent desire begins with seeing. Cf. 11. 202–10; Chaucer, *Troilus and Criseyde*, i. 271 ff., ii. 624 ff., and *C.T.*, A. 1074 ff.

18. *Strangenes*, the outpost of the lady's defences; a variant of Danger (porter in the *Roman*), and the antithesis of Belacueil ('Fair welcome') who has 'no straungenesse . . . in him sen' (Chaucerian *Romaunt of the Rose*, l. 3611). Cf. 11. 223–8.

27. *Compareson*, the lady's assessment of how far the lover falls short of the ideal. Cf. 11. 174. The word implies contempt; cf. the Scots 'Malice, discord, pryde and comparesone' (*O.E.D.*, 1535).

33. *Langour*: indifference, the antithesis of the lover's 'Bissines' (l. 60).

49. *Petie*: the traditional feminine virtue, which urges surrender to the lover to prevent him dying of unrequited or unconsummated love. Cf. 12. 172–3, note, and 31. 55.

55. *Thocht*, the lover's application in courtship; to be distinguished from Reason (11. 151–3, 199–216), a defence against falling in love.

74. The relative pronoun is often omitted in early Scots: cf. (e.g.) 11. 47 and 31. 21.

86. *Lust chasit my ladeis chalmirleir.* An apparently original way of representing possession.

87. *Gud Fame wes drownit.* See 12. 141, note.

11. *Ryght as the stern of day begouth to schyne*

The Chepman and Myllar Print is headed 'Ane litill tretie intitulit the goldyn targe'. The poem was chosen by Lindsay to exemplify Dunbar's 'language at large' (*Papyngo*, ll. 17–18). It is a more elaborate allegory of love than No. 10, using the conventional device of the dream and introducing the double company of actors familiar from the *Roman de la Rose*, Chaucer's Prologue to the *Legend of Good Women*, *The Flower and the Leaf*, and elsewhere. The stanza is that of Chaucer's 'Compleynt of Anelida'. Dunbar's theme is the failure of 'Resoun with schelde of gold' to defend him from 'Venus chevalry'. 'A mere allegorical vision, destitute of all personal or historical significance, and only designed to prove in the abstract the irresistible power of love, is capable of exciting his imagination to the highest pitch' (J. M. Ross).

2. *Vesper*, the star shining in the west before sunrise; *Lucyne*, the moon.

10. *houris*, services at set times; here, matins. Cf. l. 21. For a French description of bird-song in similar terms cf. the fourteenth-century *Messe des Oiseaus*.

16 ff.: a variation on Chaucer, *L.G.W.*, ll. 773–4.

36. *stanneris*, pebbles. Cf. Chaucer, Prologue to *C.T.*, ll. 267–8: 'His eyen twinkled . . . as doon the sterres in the frosty nyght'.

37–45. Behind the heraldic colours and artificial illumination of this setting is Dunbar's 'joy in clear water and the clear lights of Northern sun under a washed sky. . . . The transparent quality [he] gives all his lights may seem faintly unnatural to an English reader . . .; but Dunbar was a man of East Scotland, where light does give that sense of being seen through crystal' (Agnes Mure Mackenzie).

52. *merse of gold*, the round-top surrounding the lower masthead, adorned with 'mers clathes' or coloured hangings. The armorial artist Alexander Chalmers was paid ten French crowns in April 1506 for painting the merse of a royal ship (*Treasurer's Accounts*).

55. *hard on burd*, alongside the shore.

60. *kirtillis grene*, May dress. Cf. 6. 42.

61–62. *Thair brycht hairis*, &c. Conventional romance description. Cf. 12. 19–22, and Chaucer's Venus in *The Parlement of Foules*, ll. 267–8:

> Hyre gilte heres with a golden thred
> Ibounden were, untressed as she lay.

69. *Tullius*. Cicero's *De Inventione* and the *Ad Herennium* ascribed to him were among the most popular medieval textbooks of rhetoric.

73. *Thare saw I*. A stock rhetorical formula: cf. Chaucer, *C.T.*, A. 1995 ff., and *The House of Fame*, ll. 1214 ff. There is little system in Dunbar's choice of personae here or in ll. 109–26; Apollo (75) is misplaced, and Pallas duplicates Minerva (78).

79. *Lucina*, Diana; the moon.

81. *Lucifera*, the planet Venus; the morning star.

83. *sistir*, an old plural form.

87. The association of Nature with a rich gown derives ultimately from Alanus ab Insulis, *De Planctu Naturae*; also the birds and boughs welcome her (cf. ll. 94–99).

95. *Salust Nature*. Cf. Chaucer, *Parlement of Foules*, ll. 673–6.

102–5. *And to dame Venus*, &c. Cf. *The Kingis Quair*, sts. 33–35.

112. *Mars . . . armypotent*. See 7. 33, note.

119–20. *Phanus*, Faunus, deity of fields; *Janus*, deity of gates.

125–6. *Pluto the elrich incubus*, &c. Pluto is king of faery in the ME. romance of *Sir Orfeo* and in Chaucer, *C.T.*, E. 2038–41 and 2226 ff. Dunbar probably adds the emphatic 'usit no sable' to show that he knew him also as king of 'the derke pyne' (cf. *The House of Fame*, ll. 1511–12). He is probably called an incubus (demon who seeks intercourse with a woman) because of his rape of Proserpina.

145. The attacking force is made up of a number of platoons, each broadly representing a group of related feminine qualities, many of them originally personified in the *Roman de la Rose*: (i) ll. 145–50, Beauty with her supporters Fair Demeanour, Fine Appearance, Delight, and Pleasing Countenance; (ii) ll. 154–9, Youth with her characteristic qualities; (iii) ll. 160–7, Womanliness with other virtues of character—Breeding, Humility, Restraint, &c.; (iv) ll. 172–6, High Degree and qualities of rank (for Comparison see 10. 27, note); (v) ll. 182–220, Dissimulation with Physical Presence and Fair Greeting (see 10. 18, note, and *The Kingis Quair*, st. 97), Affection and Familiarity, Beauty and Acquaintance—qualities of sexual appeal. 'Hamelynes' is dramatically represented in Lindsay's *Satyre of the Thrie Estaits*, ed. Kinsley, 1954, pp. 49–50 and 57–58.

202–10. The poet's reason is no defence against the sight of his lady (cf. 10. 5, note): it is banished to the greenwood (cf. 46. 101).

223–8. *Than saw I Dangere*, &c. Deprived of Reason, the poet for a time enjoys his lady's affection; but he is rejected by a sudden reticence and thrown into despair. Cf. 10. 18, note.

253. *O reverend Chaucere*. Cf. *The Kingis Quair*, st. 197; Lydgate, *Troy Book*, ii. 4697 ff., iii. 4237 ff.

259. *oure Inglisch*: until Flodden the usual term for Scots, distinguished from Gaelic or 'Ersche'. Gavin Douglas, however, makes a distinction between 'inglis' and 'scottis', 'kepand na sudroun, but our awin langage', in the Prologue to Book I of his *Eneados* (1513).

262. *morall Gower*. Cf. *Troilus and Criseyde*, v. 1856. *Ludgate laureate*. On Dunbar's debt to Lydgate, see P. H. Nichols, *P.M.L.A.* xlvi (1931), 214–24.

271. The modest address to the book or poem has many medieval antecedents: cf. e.g. *Troilus and Criseyde*, v. 1786, and *The Kingis Quair*, st. 194.

274. 'I know that thou hast striven to show all the eloquence thou hast (but) . . . .'

12. *Apon the Midsummer evin, mirriest of nichtis*

The form and theme of this poem, entitled 'The Tretis of the Tua Mariit Wemen and the Wedo' in the Maitland MS., are discussed in the Introduction, pp. xvi–xviii. For a summary of medieval anti-feminist literature see *The Works of Chaucer*, ed. F. N. Robinson, 1933, pp. 801–2.

11. *I hard, under ane holyn.* Reporting conversation heard *en cachette* is a device used in courtly poems and popular *chansons d'aventure*.

19–20. *So glitterit*, &c. See 11. 61–62, note; cf. 11. 65–66.

23. *Curches*: a prominent and valuable part of a woman's dress, often bejewelled, and covering the head or breast. Cf. 34. 133, and *Sir Gawain and the Green Knight*, ll. 954–6:

> Kerchofes of þat on wyth mony cler perleȝ
> Hir brest and hir bryȝt þrote bare displayed,
> Schon schyrer þen snawe, þat schedes on hilleȝ.

37. *wantoun*: here perhaps 'sportive', 'given to broad jesting'; but the word may also mean 'unchaste' or 'given to amorous dalliance'.

39. *wauchtit at the wicht wyne*, 'quaffed the potent wine in large draughts'. 'Waucht' is a strong verb to use of a lady's drinking; the exposure has begun with the poet, like Pepys, 'wondering to see how the ladies did tipple'.

76. *worme*, reptile; *wobat*, the hairy oubit, caterpillar. In 'Ye blindit luvaris luke' Alexander Scott (*c.* 1550) warns against

women 'with waistit wowbattis rottin'. Wide discrepancies in age between husband and wife were common in the Middle Ages, and the aged husband is a familiar figure in comic and satiric literature. See Chaucer's *Merchant's Tale*; with ll. 83–95 *infra*, cf. *C.T.*, E. 1819–50; and with l. 126 cf. B². 1201.

96. *this amyable*, the second wife, whose answer (80 ll.) is here omitted.

100. *swanquhit*, a poetic epithet revived by Burns in 'O Mally's meek', contrasting here with *swapit of* , 'tossed off'. Cf. *supra*, l. 39, note.

109. *schene in my schrowd*, 'fair in my gown', a stock alliterative phrase. Cf. the Scots *Golagrus and Gawain* (*c.* 1470), l. 599, 'Schaip the evin to the schalk in thi schroud schene'.

118. *as tygris be terne*. Cf. Chaucer's advice in the envoy to the Clerk's Tale, 'And sklendre wyves . . . Beth egre as is a tygre yond in Ynde' (*C.T.*, E. 1198–9).

141. *ay saif my honour*: the traditional concern for reputation. Insistence on a lover's being 'secrete and sure' is a recurrent theme in the literature of *amour courtois*: 'qui non celat, non amat'. Cf. 10. 87–96, and Chaucer, *Troilus and Criseyde*, iii. 943–4:

> So werketh now in so discret a wise
> That I honour may have, and he plesaunce.

162. *within perfit eild*, 'before I was fully of age'.

168–9. *the severance wes mekle*, &c. Probably the Wedo exaggerates; she shares the Wife of Bath's preoccupation with social standing. Cf. the parson's bastard daughter 'ycomen of noble kyn' in the Reeve's Tale (*C.T.*, A. 3942–68): 'Ther dorste no wight clepen hire but "dame".'

172–3. *Bot mercy*, &c. See 10. 49, note; *infra*, ll. 213–17, note; 31. 55, where the use is again cynical. The sentiment in l. 173 recurs in Chaucer: see *C.T.*, A. 1761, and Robinson's note.

176. *I weip*, &c. Cf. the Wife of Bath, *C.T.*, D. 587–92; and the merry widow Sprutok in Henryson, *Fabillis*, st. 73.

213–17. *so law of degre*, &c. The salon for 'baronis and knychtis' is exposed as a brothel; and the Wedo whose social superiority to her husband was a source of discord satisfies her

lust where she chooses. Cf. Sensualitie in Lindsay's *Satyre*, ed.
Kinsley, p. 49:

> And ʒit I am of nature sa towart
> I lat no luiffer pas with ane sair hart.

218. *sa God*. The Print reads 'Quhen sabot all iugis'.

220. *legeand*, &c.: an ironic allusion to the saints' lives found
in Latin *Legenda*.

13. *In secreit place this hyndir nycht*

Printed in Ramsay's *Ever Green* (1724) with the title 'A Brash
[bout] of Woùing'. The poem is a concise dramatic illustration
of the attitude to *amour courtois* conventions more elaborately
expressed in No. 12 (see Introduction, pp. xvi–xviii). It follows
the tradition of the *chanson d'aventure*, in which the wooing of
a country maid by a clerkly lover is recounted in dialogue; and
it opens in courtly style with the poet *en cachette* (cf. 12. 11,
note) and the lover making his plaint against 'danger'. But
he and his 'bricht' are no more courtly lovers than are the 'tua
mariit wemen and the wedo': he is a backstairs fornicator, foul
in person and in manners (contrast Absolon in Chaucer's
Miller's Tale), and she is a giggling kitchen girl. The poem pre-
serves a comic language of endearment which has not, except
for a few phrases, survived in Scots.

23. *tuchan*, a calf's skin stuffed with straw, to encourage the
cow to give milk.

51. *golk of Marie land*, cuckoo of fairy-land, who was married
to King Berdok of Babylon, according to a burlesque tale sur-
viving in the Bannatyne MS.

14. *This nycht befoir the dawing cleir*

This comic vision has been taken as evidence that Dunbar was
at one time a friar; or—more convincingly—that he had been a
Franciscan novice wandering abroad in the guise of a friar, and
now pretends to be startled by the appearance of the habit he
had abused. Bannatyne's title is 'how dumbar wes desyrd to
be ane freir'. In the MSS. ll. 16–20 follow l. 30.

25. *Confessour*, the title which the saint bears in the Calendar,
indicating that his virtue was signalized by miracles.

34. *Kalice*, Calais; English until 1558.

38. *Derntoun*, probably Darlington, Co. Durham.

NOTES

15. *As yung Awrora with cristall haile*

Bannatyne's title is 'ane ballat of the fenyeit freir of tungland how he fell in the myre fleand to turkiland'. This and the following poem are burlesque visions, opening in conventional style and running into satire on John Damian, a 'medicinar' at court. He first appears in the *Treasurer's Accounts* for 1501 as 'Maister Johne the Franch leich'; but he 'persuadet the king of his gret cunning in al thing natural, cheiflie in that politik arte, quhilk quha knawis tha cal him an alcumist; bot his intentioun only was to milk purses' (Leslie, *Historie*, S.T.S., ii. 125). James paid him for service and equipment to pursue alchemy (see 39. 55, note). He was made Abbot of Tungland in Galloway in 1504. In 1507 he 'tuik in hand to flie with wingis', probably to regain the declining royal favour. 'The day cumis; to baith his schouders he couples his wings, that of dyvers foulis he had provydet, fra the hicht of the castel of Sterling as he wald tak jornay, he makis him to flie up in the air; bot or he was weil begun, his veyage was at an end, for this deceiver fel doun with sik a dade, that the bystanders wist not quhither tha sulde mair meine his dolour, or mervel of his dafrie. Al rinis to visit him, tha ask the Abbot with his wings how he did. He ansuers that his thich bane is brokne, and he hopet never to gang agane; al war lyk to cleive of lauchter, that quha lyk another Icarus wald now flie to hevin, rycht now lyk another Simon Magus mycht nott sett his fute to the Erde. This notable Abbot, seing himselfe in sik derisioun, to purge his crime, and mak al cleine, the wyte he lays on the wings, that tha war not uttirlie egle fethiris bot sum cok and capoune fethiris, sais he, war amang thame, nocht convenient to that use' (Leslie, op. cit., ii. 125).

4. *sonis of Sathanis seid*. The suggestion that Damian is a *diabolus* may owe something to the habit of presenting devils in feathered costume in comic scenes in the mystery plays (see A. Nicoll, *Masks, Mimes and Miracles*, 1931, p. 189).

5. *a Turk of Tartary*: a Moslem, a devil. Cf. 17. 27, note.

16. *Lumbard leid*, the medical learning of Bologna.

32. *gyans*. The association of giants and devilish practices rests upon the medieval exegesis of Gen. vi. 1-4 and Isa. xiv. 9: cf. *Beowulf*, ll. 106-13, and 46, *passim*.

51. *bruikit*, blackened with the smoke of the alchemist's furnace. Cf. Chaucer, *C.T.*, G. 663–72.

58. *quintessance*. Cf. 39. 55, note.

66. *the Menatair*, the Minotaur, half-man, half-bull. Dædalus made the maze in which it was hidden, as well as artificial wings for himself and Icarus.

68. *Saturnus*. Cf. 7. 35, note.

73. *Sanct Martynis fowle*, the martin, supposedly so named because it comes in spring and departs at Martinmas.

97–98. *The ja ... skornit him as it was lyk*: 'as was its nature to do': cf. Chaucer, *The Parlement of Foules*, l. 346, 'the skornynge jay'.

16. *Lucina schynnyng in silence of the nicht*

See No. 15, introductory note. *Lucina*, the moon.

11. *deme Fortoun*. Cf. the elaborate vision of Fortune and her wheel in *The Kingis Quair*, sts. 158–72.

31. *Saturnus*, the remotest of the planets; see 7. 35, note.

32. *Symone Magus*, a magician. See Acts, viii. 9; according to legend, he undertook to fly up to heaven, and was supported in the air by demons for a time. But at St. Peter's command they let go their hold, and he was dashed to pieces. v. p. 119 above and *Medium Ævum* xxvi, 196.

33. *Merlyne at the mone*. The moon was associated with magic and necromancy.

17. *Off Februar the fyiftene nycht*

This and the poem following are closely related in metrical form and in theme. They describe a vision of high jinks in hell on Fastern's Even, the last day of carnival before Lent. The precise dating in the first stanza suggests that the poems were written in 1507, when Fastern's Even fell on 16 February.

The motif of the Sins is often found in medieval painting, carving, and tapestry, in didactic literature and sermons, and in dramatic entertainments: see M. W. Bloomfield, *The Seven Deadly Sins*, 1952. They may have had a place in the pageants and guisings which were popular at the Scottish court. But to present this pageant in hell before an audience of devils, and throw it into the wild swirl of a dance, seem to be original notions; Dunbar revitalizes a commonplace theme by a novel blend of allegorical vision with both comedy and horror.

Each Sin has a human following: the pageant represents both sin and its consequences. The obvious relationship of sin and disease was utilized by moralists and poets alike, and Dunbar probably knew the comparisons in Gower's *Mirour de l'omme*, i. So Pryd leads his victims in a frenzy through scalding fire; the followers of Yre wound one another in madness; Envy, with whom fever and jaundice are associated, 'for pryvie hatrent . . . trymlit'; the followers of Cuvatyce and Glutteny—sins both related to dropsy—are filled up with molten gold and hot lead; the lethargy associated with Sweirnes becomes torture in the dance; and the followers of Lichery are lepers painfully linked to one another in obscene lust. (For the association of leprosy and lechery, cf. Henryson's *Testament*.) The carnival of the Sins, and the dancing pace they set, are the agony of the sinners. The scene resembles a Bedlam. But horror is dissolved in the comedy of ll. 109–20, which makes a smooth transition to the farce which follows in No. 18.

17–21. *With hair wyld bak*, &c. A portrait of a gallant. Cf. the anonymous 'Off ladies bewties to declair', ll. 41–42: 'Thair beltis thair brochis and their ringis / Makis biggingis bair at hame' (Maitland MS.).

27. *Mahoun.* Mahomet was regarded as a false god in the Middle Ages, and so his name became used for the Devil.

30. *Blak Belly and Bawsy Brown*, two fiends. Roule's *Cursing* (see 23. 77–79, note) mentions two devils named Brownie and Bellie Basie (ll. 107, 260; Maitland MS.).

31–33. *Than Yre*, &c. In de Degulleville's *Pèlerinage de la vie humaine*, translated by Lydgate and probably known to Dunbar, Wrath appears as an armed man; and in other descriptions of the Sins he is placed under the influence of Mars. *lyk a beir*. Dunbar glances at the traditional association of animals with the Sins (cf. ll. 68, 80; Bloomfield, op. cit., Appendix I). A fifteenth-century English drawing of 'saules that war dampned' shows some 'tothed as bares and thai signifie manslaers and misferers in wil or in dede and ireful' (ibid., p. 221).

56. *Rute of all evill.* 1 Tim. vi. 10.

76. *slaw of feit*. Some writers on the Sins located Sloth in the feet. Christ's wounds were sometimes interpreted as defences from the vices, and his feet were said to be nailed against Sloth.

79–80. *Lichery . . . lyk a bagit hors*. The pig and the goat are the common emblems of lust; the stallion is rarely associated with any of the Sins. But one of Dunbar's 'tua mariit wemen' (No. 12) compares her old husband to a lustful cart-horse.

108. *breif of richt*, a writ fixing a legal right to property.

113–14. *Erschemen . . . in hell*, &c. See 11. 259, note. John Major the historian remarks on the 'wild Scots' of the Highlands who 'obey more speedily their fierce and lazy chief in the doing of evil than in the working of good' (*De Gestis Scotorum*, i. 8). Dunbar elsewhere expresses a Lowland contempt for the Highlander: cf. 34. 73 and 96, [46. 127–8].

18. *Nixt that a turnament wes tryid*

In the Bannatyne MS. this poem follows No. 17 without a break. In the Maitland MS. one version opens with 17. 1–12 and 109–20, followed by 'Syn till ane turnament fast thai hyit . . .'. For the burlesque of chivalry (see ll. 22–24 and 88–96) Dunbar had a Scottish precedent in *The Taill of Rauf Coilyear* (see *Scottish Poetry*, ed. Kinsley, 1955, pp. 10–11). Lindsay continued the tradition in *The Justing betuix James Watsoun and Jhone Barbour*, which describes the struggle of two court leeches before James V at St. Andrews.

10. *beist knapparis*, biters of basting-threads (Craigie).

17. *the Greik sie*, the tideless Mediterranean.

18. *Telyouris will nevir be trew*. The unreliability of the crafts is a courtly commonplace. Cf. the anonymous 'Tak a wobster that is leill / And a myllar that will not steill' (Maitland MS.).

44–48. *Sanct Girnega*, a devil placed with Gog and Magog and Pluto in Roule's *Cursing* (Maitland MS.); introduced in *The Flytting betuix the Sowter and the Tailyour* (Bannatyne MS.) as the soutars' god, who aids them in battle by spewing 'ane pynt at a pant / Of fowll uly ba'.

85–88. This coarse comedy—of a kind which Dunbar is given to—owes something to the belief that homage is paid in the witch rites by kissing the Devil's posterior. Cf. Lindsay's *Satyre*, ed. Kinsley, p. 115.

19. *Betuix twell houris and ellevin*

An ironical 'amendis maid be him to the telyouris and sowtaris' (Bannatyne). The place and occasion are suggested by Maitland's 'Quod Dumbar quhone he drank to the Dekynnis [trades presidents] for amendis to the bodeis of thair craftis'.

20. *He that hes gold and grit riches*

11–15. 'He, on the other hand, who has a pleasing and virtuous wife (support; 'prop' also = target) suited to his disposition, and then shoots at an unknown target (i.e. goes a-whoring), and is worn out with aphrodisiacs, is the author of his own sorrow.' The Spanish fly (*cantharides*) was used as a stimulant both in medicine and in love.

22. *My heid did yak yester nicht*

9. *in my heid behind*, i.e. in the third cell of the brain, that of Memory: for similar references cf. *C.T.*, A. 1376, and Douglas, *Eneados*, Prol. i. 19–20.

23. *I that in heill wes and gladnes*

The Print ends: 'quod Dunbar quhen he wes sek etc.' The traditional title, 'Lament for the Makars', underlines only one phase in this poetic *danse macabre* (see Introduction, p. xvi). The refrain **timor mortis conturbat me** from the Office for the Dead had already been used by Lydgate in 'So as I lay this othir nyght', and in a fifteenth-century carol (R. L. Greene, *The Early English Carols*, 1935, No. 370).

37. *Art magicianis*, practitioners of the art of magic.

51. *The Monk of Bery*, John Lydgate, monk of Bury St. Edmunds.

53–55. The beginning of a roll of Scottish poets: Sir Hugh Eglinton of that ilk (d. 1377), brother-in-law of Robert II, and not otherwise known as a poet; Heryot, unknown—the Print has 'et eik Heryot', the MSS. 'Et(t)rik', which may be merely a misreading; Andro of Wyntoun, prior of Lochleven till 1422, and author of the *Oryginale Chronykil of Scotland.*

57–59. A number of poems in the Bannatyne MS. bear the attribution 'Clerk'. Afflek is unknown.

61–63. Sir Richard Holland, secretary to the Earl of Moray and author of the allegorical *Buke of the Howlat* (*c.* 1450); John Barbour, archdeacon of Aberdeen till his death in 1395, and author of *The Actes and Life of ... Robert Bruce* (1376). On these poets see *Scottish Poetry*, ed. Kinsley, 1955, pp. 2–7 and 12–13. Sir Mungo Lockhart of the Lee (d. 1489?), of Lanarkshire, is not otherwise known as a poet.

65–67. This Clerk and his work are unknown. Sir Gilbert Hay (*fl.* 1450) translated three French prose works dealing with chivalry and government, and the *Roman d'Alixandre*.

69–71. Blind Harry, to whom is attributed *The Actis and Deidis of . . . Schir William Wallace* (MS. 1488; see Kinsley, op. cit., pp. 7–10); Sandy Traill, unknown; Patrick Johnestoun, official receiver of revenues from West Lothian crown lands, producer of interludes at court in 1476–7 and 1488–9, and possibly author of *The Thre Deid Pollis* (*Poems of Henryson*, ed. H. H. Wood, 1933, pp. 205–7).

73–75. *Merseir*, probable author of a number of poems in the Bannatyne MS. Line 75 is an adaptation of Chaucer's General Prologue, l. 306.

77–79. Roull of Aberdene, unknown; Roull of Corstorphin, near Edinburgh, perhaps the author of *The cursing of Sr. Johine rowlis upoun the steilaris of his fowlis* in the Bannatyne and Maitland MSS.

81–83. Robert Henryson, 'scholmaister of Dunfermling'; Sir Johne the Ros, otherwise known only as Dunbar's supporter in the flyting with Kennedy (No. 34).

85–87. John Reid, known as Stobo, priest and secretary to James II, James III, and James IV, deceased by July 1505; Quintyne Schaw, author of a poem in the Maitland MS. and recipient of a pension of £10 in 1504.

89–91. Walter Kennedy, brother to Lord Kennedy of Dunure and a descendant of Robert III, is given a place with Chaucer, Gower, Lydgate, and Dunbar for his 'termes aureait' in Lindsay's *Papyngo* (1530). In his flyting with Dunbar (No. 34) he describes himself as 'the kingis blude, his trew speciall clerk'. Some of his poems survive in the Bannatyne and Maitland MSS.

24. *In to thir dirk and drublie dayis*

28. 'Or crave that which thou canst not keep for any length of time.'

28. *Now culit is dame Venus brand*

The contrast and conflict between fleshly and spiritual love are inevitably common themes in medieval literature. Cf. Chaucer, the end of *Troilus and Criseyde*, and Gower, envoi to *Confessio Amantis*. With the figure of Venus's fire compare Chaucer, *C.T.*, E. 1727–8, 'with hire fyrbrond . . . daunceth biforn the bryde'; Henryson, *The Testament of Cresseid*, ll. 22–35.

29. *To speik of science, craft, or sapience*

One of the two versions in the Maitland MS. ends 'Quod Dumbar at oxinfurde'. This is insufficient evidence that he was at one time a student there, or indeed that he visited the University.

9. *curious probatioun logicall*, subtle demonstration in logic.

11–12. *natural science philosophicall*, physics; *dirk . . . astronomie*, mysterious aspect of astronomy and astrology.

30. *Doverrit with dreme, devysing in my slummer*

This poem is ascribed by Bannatyne to Dunbar, but by Maitland to Sir James Inglis, 'clerk of the kingis closet' in 1512 and later Abbot of Culross, and author of 'ballattis, farses and . . . plesand playis' (Lindsay, *Papyngo*, ll. 40–42). Nothing of Inglis's writing survives for comparison, and none of the arguments advanced by Mackay Mackenzie in favour of his authorship is conclusive. Due weight must be given to the ascription in the earlier MS., and the cumulative catalogue of the poem is characteristic of Dunbar. The picture of a corrupt society anticipates Lindsay's *Satyre of the Thrie Estaits*.

14. *the deirgey* (Maitland): the Office for the Dead. Bannatyne has 'the Psalme and Testament to reid', which misses the internal rhymes and is one of several protestant emendations found in this MS.

19. *losin sarkis*, garments with lozenge-shaped insertions; *glengoir*, the pox, rampant at this time. In 1497 the king's

council ordered sufferers from the disease to be carried to the island of Inchkeith, in the Forth, 'thair to remane quhill God prouyde for thair health' (Edinburgh Burgh Records).

31. *mycharis*: Maitland. Bannatyne has the inappropriate 'murdereris'.

48. 'So many concerned for rank and so few for the common weal.' Cf. the complaint of Iohne the Common-weill in Lindsay's *Satyre*, ed. cit., pp. 125–6.

57. *halland schekkaris*: beggars, shakers of the *hallan*, the draught-screen between the door and the fire. *Cowkelbyis gryce*: *Colkelbie's Sow* is a farcical popular verse tale of a feast. See T. F. Henderson, *Scottish Vernacular Literature*, 1910, pp. 85–90.

62. *cursing*, coursing over growing crops.

66. *ketchepillaris*, tennis-court keepers. The tennis of the time was a hand-game (*jeu de paume*) played in a covered court. Dunbar's condemnation of sport seems harsh; but compare Lindsay's parson, who is expert at tennis, foot-ball, 'the carts, the tabils and the dyse', 'thocht I preich not' (*Ane Satyre*, ed. cit., p. 159).

67. *tutivillaris*, tattlers: cf. *Colkelbie's Sow*, l. 61, 'a tuttivillus, a tutlar'. Titivillus, originally a devil supposed to collect words mumbled or dropped out in the service and hold them in hell against the unfortunate priest, became a figure in the mystery plays.

73. *fowill tailis*, fashionable trains which dragged in the mud. A verse supplication was presented later by Lindsay *In Contemptioun of Syde Taillis*, 'Quhilk throw the dust and dubbis traillis / Thre quarteris lang behind thare heillis'.

76. *kittie*: a wench, whore. Lindsay's Placebo cynically suggests asking the Prioress 'gif it be sin to tak ane Kaity' (*Ane Satyre*, ed. cit., p. 48).

78. *apill renye*. Obscure. Mackay Mackenzie plausibly explains it as an aromatic box in the shape of an orange (*apil oranye*), carried at the neck or the waist on a chain.

31. *Ane murlandis man of uplandis mak*

In the Bannatyne MS., one of 'certane ballattis aganis the vyce in sessioun court and all estaitis'. The Court of Session, originating in the 'Session' established in 1426 by James I to deal with all cases cognizable by the king's council, is the supreme civil tribunal of Scotland.

5. *undir confessioun*, under the seal of confession. Probably at this time, as later, the public was not allowed to hear the proceedings of this court, and those present were sworn not to reveal them.

29–31. 'Some interpret writs (issued by the court under the royal signet) and some make objections ('exceptionis and causis defensall') to the court's ruling; some stand aside and pick up the incidental pronouncements of the lawyers; some cases are adjourned, some win, and some lose.'

41. *the sait*, the court. Cf. Scott, *The Heart of Midlothian*, iii: 'A lord of seat—a lord of Session'.

45. *Carmeleitis and Cordilleris*: the White Friars, deriving from a twelfth-century colony on Mount Carmel, and the Franciscan Grey Friars, who wore girdles of knotted cord.

50. *he complexioun*, vigorous constitution.

55. *All mercyfull wemen thair eirandis grantis*. See 10. 49 and 12. 172–3, notes.

32. *Quhy will ye marchantis of renoun*

The medieval city of Edinburgh extended east down the long high ridge from the Castle, through the Lawnmarket and the High Street, to the burgh of Canongate and Holyrood Palace. The houses, generally wood-framed with a plaster infilling, stood often at right angles to the street; and temporary booths, erected against the gables, lined the thoroughfare. The old Tolbooth, where the Parliament and Court of Session met, stood to the west of St. Giles' Kirk, leaving a narrow street between the Lawnmarket and the High Street. To the east the Luckenbooths, or permanent shops, ran down to the head of the High street. The commercial quarter of the city was crammed and odoriferous.

15. *stinkand scull*. Reidpeth's transcript has 'scull' altered from 'stull', which is probably a scribal error caused by 'styll' (see l. 38, note). The school has not been identified. The 'summa scola grammatica', now the Royal High School, was at this time situated in Kirk o' Field Wynd, well to the south of the 'parroche kirk' of St. Giles. The 'stinkand scull' may have been part of the ecclesiastical establishment.

22. *hie croce*: the Mercat Cross, to the north-east of St. Giles'. It was rebuilt in 1555 and 1617. The present Cross is a Victorian replacement incorporating part of the old shaft.

24. *trone*; the site of the king's 'tron', or public weighing machine, also used as a pillory.

30. *Now the day dawis*, a popular song, transformed into a pious one in *The Gude and Godlie Ballatis* at the Reformation. Cf. Douglas, 'Proloug of the Threttene Buik of Eneados', 'menstrallis playing The joly day now dawis'. *Into Joun* has not been identified.

31. *Sanct Cloun*: Cluanus, a sixth-century Irish abbot, invoked before eating and drinking in Lindsay's *Satyre* (ed. cit., pp. 88 and 189).

38. *stinkand styll*, probably the Old-Kirk Style, an alley through the Luckenbooths.

39. *hamperit in ane hony came*, cramped like bees in a honey comb.

57–59. 'Since the countryside resorts to this town because the king's court and the Court of Session (see No. 31, note) are here . . . .'

33. *Airlie on As Wodnisday*

'A curious picture from the life, in the style of Flemish paintings' (Pinkerton). Cf. 'Good gossip mine', *The Early English Carols*, ed. Greene, No. 419. *As Wodnisday*, the first day of Lent.

34. *Schir Johine the Ros, ane thing thair is compild*

This is the earliest surviving example in Scots of a literary *flyting* —a blend of primitive literary criticism and lampoon apparently popular in fifteenth- and sixteenth-century Scotland. The antecedents of the form are obscure: neither the old French types of verse disputation nor the invectives of the humanists provide good analogues. But the relation of early Scots flyting to medieval bardic contests in Gaelic verse has yet to be worked out (see James Ross, 'Gaelic folk-song', *Scottish Studies*, i (1957), 119–21). The flyting of Dunbar and Kennedy is not the only evidence of lively dispute among Scottish literati: Dunbar elsewhere rails against one Mure, who 'indorsit myn indyting/ With versis off his awin hand wryting', and Gavin Douglas, in his *Eneados*, remarks 'detractouris intil every place' who 'or evir thay reidis the wark, biddis burn the buik'.

The flyting of Dunbar and Kennedy may have developed in a series of attacks and counter-attacks circulated in manuscript at court; it may, at least in its final form, have been read before the king as a formal duel in verse. As it survives, it consists of Dunbar's initial challenge (ll. 1–24) and Kennedy's counter-challenge (threatening reprisals if 'evir I heir ocht of your making mair'), and a sustained piece of vituperation from each poet. Part of Dunbar's contribution is reprinted here.

On Walter Kennedy see 23. 89–91, note. His kinsman and 'commissar' Quinting, or Quintene, is a ghost now, though Lindsay in 1530 placed him among the dead whose 'libellis bene levand' (*Papyngo*, ll. 19–20). Cf. 36. 37–38. Of Dunbar's 'commissar', John the Ross, nothing is known (cf. 23. 83).

17. *baird*, strolling minstrel; used derogatively. In Dunbar's time laws were in force against 'vagabundis, fulis, bardis, scudlaris, and siclyk idill pepill'. Cf. ll. 111 and 120.

26. *dagone*, villain; originally the deity of the Philistines (see Milton, *Paradise Lost*, i. 457–66).

37–38. *Thow purpest*, &c. Dunbar is probably referring to some court incident, not accusing Kennedy of attempted poisoning.

51–54. St. Lawrence was martyred in 258 by being burnt on a gridiron. The allusion to the execution of St. John (? Baptist) is obscure. Bellenden in his history (1536) repeats the traditional story of the English who, disliking the preaching of Augustine of Canterbury, 'dang him with skait rumpillis': 'God tuke on thaim sic vengeance, that thay and thair posteritie had lang talis mony yeris eftir'. St. Bartholomew is said to have been flayed alive and crucified while on a missionary journey in Armenia.

62. *Karrik*, in southern Ayrshire.

71. *wathman weid* (Maitland), a common phrase. Bannatyne's reading, 'wachmanis weid', is inferior.

73. *Ersche katherene*, Highland reiver. See 11. 259 and 17. 113–14, notes. Dunbar's reflections on Kennedy's Gaelic ancestry are countered by Kennedy's praise of 'Irische . . . all trew Scottis mennis lede', once 'the gud langage of this land'— a doctrine still preached.

99. *saffrone*, used as a cordial.

100. *Gy*: Guido de Corvo, whose spirit haunted his wife and was ultimately exorcized by four Dominican friars. Cf. 46. 14.

117. *rubbit quheit*, wheat rubbed in the hands to extract the grain. Earlier in his flyting Dunbar describes Kennedy as 'fane at evin for to bring hame a single [handful of grain], / Syne rubbit at ane uthir auld wyvis ingle'.

121. *Strait Gibbonis air*. In 1503 a payment was made to 'Strait ('strict'? 'stingy') Gibbon' by royal command; he was possibly a court jester.

131. *lyk ane howlat chest with crawis*. Cf. 15. 69 ff.

133. *Keip curches in the merk*, 'hide your finery'. See 12. 23, note.

145. *Hilhous*, Sir John Sandilands of Hillhouse. The reference is obscure.

35. *Sir Jhon Sinclair begowthe to dance*

The version in the Maitland MS. ends 'Quod dumbar of a dance in the quenis chalmer'; and the poem illustrates the personalities and manners of the queen's retinue. Sir John Sinclair appears frequently in the *Treasurer's Accounts* from 1490 onwards, playing bowls and cards with the king, and he was in the queen's service till Flodden. Robert Shaw was a court physician, and prescribed for the queen's 'bleding of the nes' in February 1504–5; he became a priest in 1508. The 'maister almaser' may be the Englishman Dr. Babington, who was concerned in the queen's marriage arrangements in 1503, remained in Scotland as her almoner, and was dead by 1507. He was nominated to the deanery of Aberdeen in December 1505. John Bute appears in the records from November 1506. Mistress Musgraeffe has not been identified, though she may have been the wife of Sir John Musgrove, who came from England with the queen. Dounteboir seems to have been a general name for a lady in waiting. On James Dog see No. 37, note.

13. *Stranaver*: Strathnaver in Sutherland, named as a remote place. Cf. 42. 5.

36. *Now lythis off ane gentill knycht*

A parody of the romances, using the romance stanza and conventional tags and diction as Chaucer had done in the Tale of

Thopas, and following Chaucer's example in the comic turn of the short line and in the allusions to 'faerie'. Norny was a member of the royal household. Editors have supposed him to be a jester; but although he is 'lord of evere full', the one thing he lacks is the jester's bells. Baxter plausibly suggests that he was 'a braggart, whom Dunbar skilfully ridiculed as *miles gloriosus*'.

12. *Rois and Murray land*, conveniently remote. Norny was in the north with the king late in 1505.

16. *Quhettane*, Chattan: a clan which 'hevely trublit' the north, and was one of the combatants in the battle of the clans at Perth in 1396. See the close of Scott's *Fair Maid of Perth*, and his note xiv.

19–24. It was conventional to recount a knight's accomplishments: but 'werslingis' were hardly more appropriate to a Scottish knight in 1505 than to an English knight in the fourteenth century (cf. the Tale of Thopas, st. 5). Significantly, Norny's victories were not at court, but 'upaland'; he is a provincial champion.

25–30. The conventional comparison with acknowledged heroes (cf. the Tale of Thopas, st. 29); but *Robein under bewch* and the others from Sherwood are heroes of popular balladry, not of chivalric romance. *Roger off Cleckniskleuch*, unidentified, was presumably associated with Robin Hood. *Gy off Gysburne* was an ally of the Sheriff of Nottingham, slain by Robin Hood. There survive a ballad on the episode, and a fragmentary dramatic piece dating from *c.* 1475. *Allan Bell* is probably Adam Bell, the hero of the ballad 'Mery it was in grene forest'. *Simonis sonnes off Quhynfell* are unidentified; but a dance with this name is mentioned in *Colkelbie's Sow* (see 30. 57, note).

Municipal pageants, in Scotland as elsewhere, were conducted under the command of a lord of misrule, who sometimes gave place to Robin Hood or Little John imported from the south (cf. 46. 137–44); but in 1555 the puritanical Estates 'ordanit that in all tymis cumming na maner of persoun be chosin Robert Hude nor Lytill Johne, Abbot of vnressoun, Quenis of Maij nor vtherwyse, nouther in Burgh nor to landwart in ony tyme to cum' (see A. J. Mill, *Medieval Plays in Scotland*, 1927, pp. 21–33).

35. *Sir Bevis*, hero of a fourteenth-century English romance; cf. Chaucer, *C.T.*, B². 2089.

37. *Quenetyne*. See No. 34, introductory note. He may have written an earlier skit on Norny.

43. *Curris kneff*, a mere assistant to the court fool Curry, who, with his wife Daft Anne of Linlithgow, seems to have turned folly to comfortable profit in the king's service.

37. *The wardraipper of Venus boure*

'Quod dunbar of Iames dog kepair of the quenis wardrep' (Maitland). Dog had been groom of the king's wardrobe. He passed into the queen's service in a position of great responsibility, with the charge of furnishings, tapestries, and the like as well as liveries, and the control of payments in kind to court servants; and he evidently remained in this post at least until 1527. 'The Queen seems to have ordered Dunbar a doublet . . . but Mr. Doig, having scrupled, was *hitched into a rime*, and thus stands as a skeleton in the Surgeons Hall of Fame' (Pinkerton).

5. *markis*: device, seal. Margaret's letter-seal shows her crowned, seated, 'before her a hound or brachet leaping up' (British Museum *Catalogue of Seals*, 14899).

19. *Gog-ma-gog*, chief of the giants of Albion destroyed by Brute when he came to Britain with the Trojan remnant. Cf. 46. 37; Spenser, *The Faerie Queene*, III. ix. 50.

38. *O gracious princes, gud and fair*

'Quod dunbar of the said Iames quhen he had plesett him' (Maitland). 'If so, whether was it most dangerous to displease, or to please Dunbar?' (Pinkerton).

4. *na dog*. See 37. 5, note.

39. *Schir, ye have mony servitouris*

One of Dunbar's occasional remonstrances on the king's neglect of his poet, and a vivid picture of the activity of town and court. The cumulative catalogue is a common stylistic device in both his satiric and his reflective verse.

7. *Men of armes*, &c. Cf. No. 8, note. Of James's court, says Lindsay (*Papyngo*, ll. 500–504),

> throuch Europe sprang the fame
> Of lustie Lordis and lufesum Ladyis ying;
> Tryumphand tornayis, justyng and knychtly game,
> With all pastyme accordyng for ane kyng.

9. *Musicianis . . . and mirrie singaris.* James loved musical entertainment. He himself played the lute and monochord, and he had an organ carried on royal progresses. 'After mass,' says Ayala, 'he has a cantata sung.' He encouraged country singers liberally—'wemen . . . about simmer treis singand' was another pleasant custom put down at the Reformation. On New Year's Day 1507 payment was 'giffin to divers menstrales, schawmeris, trumpetis, taubronaris, fithelaris, lutaris, harparis, clarscharis, piparis, extending to lxix persons'; and the *Treasurer's Accounts* mention also, in the same year, minstrels from France, Ireland, England, and Italy, Italian pipers, guisers and dancers, singers, and a 'Franch quhissillar'. *Chevalouris* (10) ev. = entertainers.

12. *Beildaris of barkis.* On 13 August 1506 James wrote to Louis XII: 'For a long time past we have been busy with the building of a fleet for the protection of our shores. . . . Since there is a greater abundance of building material in your realm, we have sent our men thither to fetch beams and oakwood from a friendly nation, and to bring shipwrights to us. . . . Order this fleet, me and my people, whither you will; you will find no one readier to obey, either for vow or honour' (Gregory Smith, *The Days of James IV*, pp. 103–4). His finest achievement in ship-building was the *Great Michael*, which 'wasted a' the wuids of Scotland to big her, and danged a' the men in Scotland to launch her'. She was, says Pitscottie, 'the greattest scheip and maist of strength that ever saillit in Ingland or France . . . Scho was xij scoir of futtis of length and xxxv futte withtin the wallis; scho was ten fute thik in the waill, cuttit jeastis of aik witht hir wallis and burdis on everie syde sa stark and thik that na canon could gang throw hir' (*Historie*, i. 251). She carried a ship's company of 300, with 120 gunners and 'ane thowsand men of weir'. There is a reconstruction of the *Michael* in the Royal Scottish Museum.

16. *Pryntouris*: perhaps, in the older sense, coiners; but Dunbar more probably refers to the printing press of Chepman and Myllar set up by royal charter in 1507. Chepman and Myllar undertook 'to furnis and bring hame ane prent' from France, 'and expert men to use the samyne', to print the laws and acts, chronicles, mass-books, legends of Scottish saints and other books. The surviving prints of *c.* 1508 are the earliest dated Scottish books. See Note on the text, p. xxi.

potingaris, apothecaries, employed as alchemists. See l. 55, note.

41. *gunnaris.* James's artillery, French and Scots, was celebrated for its variety and quality. The artillery of the *Great Michael* was particularly 'great and costlie to the king', with 35 cannon and 'iij c schott of small artaillyie', 'hagbut and cullvering, corsebowis and handbowis' (Pitscottie, *Historie*, i. 251). The artillery experts are probably included in Dunbar's catalogue as intruders like the foreigners in ll. 42–43: there are references in the *Treasurer's Accounts* for 1507–13 to foreign gunners—'George the Almane gunnar', 'Hannis', 'Wolf', and Frenchmen—who received payments of drinksilver and taffeta and hose.

42. *clarat cunnaris,* connoisseurs of claret, the staple Scottish wine until the introduction in the eighteenth century of 'that other liquor called port' (David Hume). There were Frenchmen of every rank at court, from noblemen to gardeners, priests to minstrels, doctors to shipwrights and blacksmiths.

43. *Innopportoun askaris of Yrland kynd.* Irishmen mentioned in the *Treasurer's Accounts* include friars and priests, a falconer, a lathenar, a lorimer, minstrels, and the obscure beneficiaries, 'the Irland men'.

55. *ingynouris joly,* alchemists. James zealously collected books and materials for the study of alchemy. The *Treasurer's Accounts* show expenses incurred in 'bigging of . . . the furnes for *quinta essencia*' and equipping the 'potingaris' Mosman and Foular. The charlatan Damian (see No. 15, introductory note) 'causet the king to believe that he, be multiplyinge and utheris his inventions, wold make fine gold of uther mettall, quhilk science he callit the quintassence; quhairupon the king maid greit cost, bot all in vaine' (Bishop Leslie).

56. *multiplie,* increase the precious metals by transmutation of the baser metals.

66. *Colkelbeis gryce.* See 30. 57, note.

85. *lat the vennim ische.* Cf. 34. 9–16.

40. *Schir, for your grace bayth nicht and day*

An address to the king, asking him to accept the queen's petition on Dunbar's behalf. *Johne Thomsounis man,* a fellow who yields to the wishes of his wife (Joan). Cf. Scott, *Old Mortality,* xxxviii: 'D'ye think I am to be John Tamson's man, and maistered by women a' the days o' my life?'

19. On the custom of vowing a knightly deed to the swan at a feast see *The Buik of Alexander*, S.T.S., 1. xxxviii–xl.

21–24. *The mersy*, &c. See No. 5, introductory note.

41. *Schir, yit remembir as of befoir*

22. *dandely, bischop,* possibly a nursery song.

29. *ballattis undir the byrkis*, love-songs and light poems.

34. *He playis*, &c. 'He gets all in this game of chance, I get nothing.' A *totum* was a four-sided disk made for a spinning toy, with a letter inscribed on each side: T (*totum*), A (*aufer*), D (*depone*), N (*nihil*, 'nichell'). The player's fortune was set by the letter uppermost when the toy fell.

42. *Schir, lett it nevir in toun be tald*

An address to the king. The *Respontio Regis* is doubtless the work of James himself: in Reidpeth's transcript of the Maitland MS. (which now preserves only ll. 1–31) 'Q: dumbar' follows l. 68.

2. *Yuillis yald*. The humour of the poem derives from this special use of 'yald', an old horse, to denote anyone who was not wearing a new garment at Christmas. Payments were made to Dunbar on 27 January 1505–6 'for caus he wantit his goun at Yule' and on 4 January 1506–7 'in recompensatioun for his goun' (*Treasurer's Accounts*). The phrase survived until recently in Aberdeenshire as *eelshard*. The term *paseyad* indicates a similar custom at Easter. See A. S. C. Ross in the *Saga-Book* of the Viking Society, xii.

5. *Strenever*. The Maitland MS. has 'streneverne'. Cf. 35. 13, note. *strenthis* = (barren) fastnesses.

36. *knawin*: MS. 'knawit', but the rhyme is with *yald*.

43. *I, Maister Andro Kennedy*

'The tesment of maister andro kennedy maid be dumbar quhen he wes lyk to dy' (Bannatyne). Kennedy was apparently a drunken court physician. Clerk (l. 33) may have been a rival; but see 23. 57.

Dunbar manages an echo of the great twelfth-century *Confessio*—

> Meum est propositum in taberna mori,
> ut sint vina proxima morientis ori....

But his intention is comic; and he tries the popular burlesque exercise of writing in two languages. His alternate lines in Scots and Latin are not precisely macaronic, except on occasion (cf. ll. 4 and 62): a more orthodox example is Drummond of Hawthornden's (?) *Polemomiddinia*, in which vernacular words are given Latin terminations and worked into a Latin context. For the poetic testament Dunbar had models in Villon, and in parodies of Villon. L. 56 is from Ps. ci. 10, l. 58 from the hymn sung in the Funeral Mass. For l. 68 see Ps. cxviii. 73.

4. Cf. Chaucer, *C.T.*, D. 873 ff.

12. *Na blind Allane*, &c. A proverbial expression.

24. *sueit Cuthbert*, evidently the keeper of the cellar.

40. *Scribendo dentes*, &c. Obscure: the clue presumably lies in 'entes'.

44. *Ade*, Adam.

44. *We that ar heir in hevins glory*

'Dirige to the king, bydand ouir lang in stirling' (Maitland). James sometimes retired to the Franciscan house at Stirling. 'Dirige' is the opening word of the antiphon at Matins in the Office for the Dead: the poem is a parody—and its conclusion an adaptation—of parts of that Office, contrasting the purgatorial austerity of the Franciscans with the celestial delights of the Edinburgh court. The poet and his fellows are represented as an apostle and a heavenly choir.

52. *every fische that swymis*. 'It is impossible', says Ayala, 'to describe the immense quantity of fish. The old proverb says already *piscinata Scotia*. Great quantities of salmon, herring, and a kind of dried fish . . . are exported. The quantity is so great that it suffices for Italy, France, Flanders, and England.'

55. *clairettis*. See 39. 42, note.

56. *Angers and . . . Orliance*, Angers and Orleans on the Loire.

45. *My gudame wes a gay wif, bot scho wes ryght gend*

This poem appears without ascription in an early print, after Nos. 12 and 23 and before No. 43; and there is no ascription in the Bannatyne MS. Mackay Mackenzie thought it remarkable that if No. 45 was known to be Dunbar's, neither source should have said so. But only Nos. 12 and 23 are given as Dunbar's in the print—No. 43 ends 'Explicit'; and Bannatyne's ignorance of the authorship of No. 45 is not an argument against Dunbar. The controlled fantasy of the poem, moreover, and the comically novel application of the romance stanza, are characteristic of Dunbar as of no other Scots poet of his time.

3. *Kyttok*: a familiar or disrespectful term for a woman.

4. *like a caldrone cruke, cler under kell*: grotesque realism and a romance tag in comic juxtaposition.

46. *Harry, harry, hobbillschowe*

The title of this piece in the Asloan MS. is 'The manere of the crying of ane playe'; in the Bannatyne MS., 'Ane litill interlud of the droichis [dwarf's] part of the play'. The poem is anonymous in Bannatyne, and the end of the earlier Asloan version is missing. But the metre and the quality of the comic fantasy suggest Dunbar.

This is the only surviving example of a 'cry' to the May play, celebrating the summer festival (see Mill, *Mediaeval Plays in Scotland*, pp. 19–35). If Bannatyne's title is accurate, the allusions to the player's giant kind are calculated dramatic farce.

1. *Harry, harry, hobbillschowe*: 'Help! uproar!'; a cry for silence.

5. *A soldane owt of Seriand land*: a Syrian sultan, a pagan devil. Cf. 15. 5, note.

10. *blynd Hary*: the one-eyed ancient of folk-tale, derived from Odin, and endowed with supernatural knowledge . See Mackay Mackenzie's Appendix D and *R.E.S.*, N.S., viii (1957), 24–26.

14. *the spreit of Gy*. See 34. 100, note.

16. *Licht as the lynd*: the usual simile is 'as leif on lynd'.

33. *Fyn McKowle*, a legendary Gaelic hero: 'the sonne of Coelus, Scottisman; . . . ane man of huge statoure, of xvii cubitis of hicht. He was ane gret huntar, and richt terribill, for his huge quantitie, to the pepill: of quhome ar many vulgar fabillis amang us, nocht unlike to thir fabillis that are rehersit of King Arthure' (Bellenden, *Croniklis*, vii. 18). Lindsay's Pardoner offers the people 'ane relict lang and braid, / Of Fine Macoull the richt chaft blaid' (*Ane Satyre*, ed. Kinsley, p. 112).

37. *Gog Magog.* See 37. 19, note.

62. *Cragorth,* Craigforth near Stirling.

67–68. A reference to the raising of the wind by witches, first mentioned in Higden, *Polychronicon.* Witches are often located in Norway or Lapland.

81. *mekle Gow Makmorne*: Goll Mac Morna, slayer of Cumhal, the leader of the rival Fianna and father of Finn.

101. *under the lynd,* to the woods: cf. 11. 202–10.

111. *Sanct Gelis*: St. Giles' Kirk, Edinburgh.

113. *Sophea*: the 'Grand Sophy', Shah of Persia.

116. *turn to Turky.* Cf. 15. 5–6.

117. Probably a reference to the invasion of Lombardy by Louis XII in 1509.

121. *Swetherik,* Sweden.

127–8. *For never,* &c. Dunbar's sentiment. Cf. 17. 113–14, note.

140. *grene lufraye.* Cf. 6. 42, note.

141. *Robyn Hude,* king of the May game. See 36. 25–30, note.

165. The MSS. seem defective. The Asloan version ends unsatisfactorily at line l. 165; Bannatyne ends with ll. 166–73, but omits ll. 161–5.

GLOSSARY

THIS glossary includes words now obsolete or only dialectal, words in difficult spelling, and words used by Dunbar in obsolete or special senses. It does not contain words explained in the notes. The following variations in spelling should be noted: *a* varies with e, i, o, ai, au, aw; *e* with a, i, ie, ei, eu, ew, ey; *i* with a, e, y; *o* with a, u, ou, ow, oy, ui; *u* with o, w, ou, ow, ui; *c* with k.

Plural nouns end in *-is*, *-ys*. When a personal pronoun accompanies the present indicative of the verb, the 2nd person singular *only* ends in *-is*; in other circumstances *all* persons end in *-(i)s*. The present participle ends in *-and*, *-ing*, *-yng*, and the gerund in *-ing*, *-yng*. The past participle and past of weak verbs often end in *-it*, *-yt*; the past participle of strong verbs ends in *-in*, *-yn*.

A full account of the orthography and grammar of early Scots is given in G. Gregory Smith, *Specimens of Middle Scots*, 1902.

Words identical in form but different in meaning and origin are usually put under a single headword and the senses distinguished by arabic numerals.

a, aw, (1) all, (2) one, a.
a per se, paragon, excellence.
abak, back.
abasit, dismayed, confounded.
abayd, delay.
ab(b)eit, abyte, habit, dress.
aboif, abufe, above.
aboin, abone, above.
abusioun, abuse.
accord, suit.
addrest, prepared.
adir, either.
adjutorie, help, helper.
aep, aip, ape.
aferit, affeird, afraid.
affeir, manner, appearance, bearing.
affrey, fear, alarm; affrayit, frightened.
afoir, before.

agane, agayn, again, against, in return.
aganis, against, in preparation for.
ail(l), ale.
air, heir.
air, airlie, early.
aitis, oats.
aix, axe.
akword, ill-tempered, perverse.
alane, allane, alone.
albeid, although.
ald, auld, old (one).
alkin, allkin, of every kind.
all, entirely.
allevin, ? without exception.
allowit, praised.
almaser, almoner.
als, also, as.
amene, delightful, pleasant.

amyable, friendly, lovable.
anarmit, in arms.
and, and, if.
ane, a, one, only.
anis, (1) once, (2) asses.
anker, anchor.
an(n)amalit, enamelled, enriched.
annuche, enough.
anteris, adventures.
a(u)nter(o)us, adventurous.
apill, apple; ~ rubye, a variety of apple.
applyit, attached, inclined.
arayit, arreyit, prepared.
arrest, (v.) seize, (n.) durance.
artelyie, artilye, artillery.
as, ash(es).
ask, newt, eft.
assay, assault, attempt.
assege, maid, beleaguered.
astrologgis, astrologers.
at under, beneath.
atour, attour, over, beyond, besides.
atteir, attire.
attemperit, mild.
aucht, (v.) owed, ought, (n.) possession.
aupone, upon.
availye, avail.
aventur, chance, fortune; adventure.
aver, avir, cart-horse.
awalk, awake; pa. t. awoi(l)k.
awin, awne, own.
awp, bullfinch.

bab, babe.
babill, jester's bauble.
bachilleris, young men.
bae, baa.
bagit hors, stallion.
baid; endured, remained.
bailfull, sorrowful.
ba(i)r, (1) boar, (2) bore, carried, (3) bare.
baird, bard, minstrel.
bald, bauld, bawld, bold, fierce.
ballat, ballet, poem, song.
ballingar, small ship.

balmit, anointed.
bancat, banquet.
bandoun, dominion, authority.
bane, bone.
barat, barrat, strife, distress.
barganer, quarreller, wrangler.
bark, ship.
barkit, tanned, hardened.
barne, child; ~heid, childhood, childishness.
barres, enclosure, lists.
Bartane, Bertane, Britain.
batalrus, warlike.
ba(w)d, asked for; bade.
bawis, testicles.
bawsy, coarse, clumsy.
be, by, by the time that, when; ~ sic thre, three times.
be(c)k, bow, nod.
beclip, embrace.
bedene, at once, soon, altogether.
bedirtin, dirtied.
bedret, fouled.
bedroppit, spattered.
befoir, beforne, before.
beft, beat, buffeted.
befyld, befouled.
begouth, begowth(e), began.
beidis, rosary.
beildar, builder.
bein(e), is; p.p. been.
beir(e), (1) barley, (2) bear, (3) boar, (4) uproar.
beis, shalt be.
bekis, corner teeth.
bellamy, fair friend.
belly huddr(o)un, big belly, glutton.
belyf, at once.
bendit, stretched, swelled, excited.
benigne, bening, benyng, mild.
benignite, mildness, gentleness.
benner, banner.
berand, neighing.
berd, (1) bird, (2) beard.
berevit, snatched away.
beriall, beryl; crystal-clear.
be(y)rne, man, fellow.
beschittin, covered in excrement.

beseik, beseech.

besein, besene, arrayed.

bespew, foul with vomit.

besyde, besides, as well; near by.

betuix, between.

beuche, bewche, bough; *pl.* bewis.

bewrie, reveal.

bicker, bikker, (*v.*) assail; (*n.*) assault.

bid, offer, desire (to).

bill, letter, document.

billie, companion, sweetheart.

birn(e), burn.

birst, burst.

bissart, buzzard.

bla, livid.

blaiknit, made pale.

blandit, connected.

blasing, shining with colour.

blaw, blow; blawin owt, spread abroad.

ble, complexion.

blek, leather blacking stain.

blenk, glance.

blent, looked.

bler, blear (the eye), hoodwink.

blew out on, denounced.

blomyt, covered with flowers.

blyn, cease.

bo, mock, make a face.

bocht, bought.

bodin, arrayed, furnished.

bogill, spectre, goblin.

bony, fine, pretty.

borrow, surety; God to ~, in God's name; borrowit, ransomed, redeemed.

bost, threat.

bosteous, busteous, bustuos, rough, violent, hostile.

bot, but, except, only, without.

botingis, boots.

boun, go, prepare; *p.p.* ready.

bour(e), bower.

bourd(e), jest; bourdour, jester.

bowgle, wild ox.

bowk, body.

braid, bred, start.

bra(e)k, bre(i)k, break; *pa. t.* brak.

brallar, brawler.

brand, (1) sword, weapon, (2) torch, (3) brawned, developed.

brandeist, swaggered.

brane, bran.

brattill, rattling noise.

brattis, wretched children, *or* ragged garments (30. 39).

brayd, broad.

brayis, braes, hills.

bred, broad. See also braid.

breid, (1) bread, (2) breed.

breid, breadth, width; on ~, abroad, widely, open.

breif, breve, (*v.*) write, tell; (*n.*) writ.

breik, breeches.

bre(i)k. See bra(e)k.

bremys, bream, fish.

brethir, brethren.

bricht, (*a.*) bright; (*n.*) fair lady.

brim, brym, fierce, furious.

brint, burnt.

brist, burst.

brodir, brother.

broud, embroidered.

browderit, embroidered.

bruik, bruke, enjoy, make use of.

bruikit, streaked with black.

brukill, brukle, brittle, frail.

brybour, vagabond, thief.

brydallis, wedding feasts.

brylyoun, (obscure).

bukky, shell; (*fig.*) protuberance in the cheek.

bumbard, bumbart, (*adj.*) idle; (*n.*) drone.

bundin, bound.

bung, barrel stopper.

burch(t), burgh, town.

burd, board; ~claith, tablecloth.

bure, bore, carried.

busk, deck out, dress.

bussome, broom, of heather or birch.

but. See bot.

bute, (1) profit, remedy, (2) boot.

buthman, shopkeeper, merchant.

by, beside, near; past; in addition (to).

byd, remain, (a)wait.
byrk, birch.
byt(tar), bite(r).

cager, carrier, hawker.
cair, sorrow, melancholy.
cairt, cart, (1) card, (2) cart.
cald, caïld, cawld, cold.
cale, broth, soup.
calling, greeting.
calsay, paving, paved street.
campio(u)n, champion.
cannoun, channoun, canon, the
central portion of the Mass.
capirculyoun, capercaillie, wood-
grouse (Gaelic).
caprowsy, hooded cape.
carefull, dreadful.
carl(e), peasant, fellow (of little
worth), old man.
carling, karling, old woman.
carp, discourse, talk.
carrybald, wild man.
cartane, quartan.
cary, move.
cassin, cassyne, cast (aside), dis-
used.
catherein, katherene, cateran.
catt nois, snub nose.
catyve, villain, wretch.
cawandar, (obscure).
cawkit, defecated.
celicall, heavenly, divine.
celsitud, eminence, exaltation.
chaft, jaw.
chaip, escape.
chaist, chest, chased. See chaste.
chalmer, chamber, closet; ~leir,
chamberlain, steward.
channoun. See cannoun.
char, on, ajar, open.
chassand, chasing.
chaste, chest, chaste (= impo-
tent).
cheir, chere, countenance, de-
meanour, mood, feeling.
cheis, choose.
cheny(i)e, che(y)ne, chain.
cherarchy, hierarchy, heavenly
host.

chest. See chaist.
chevis, achieve, acquire.
chittirlilling, (obscure).
choip, jaw.
chois, the best, 'flower'.
choll, jowl.
chuf, churl.
chuk, chuck, bob under the
chin.
chymys, mansion, manor-house,
dwelling.
claif, pa.t. split; clove.
clairett, claret.
claith, cloth; clais, clay(th)is,
clothes.
clap, draw; caress, fondle.
clarefeid, polished.
clasch, strike, clap noisily.
clatterar, chatterer, tattler.
claver, clever, clover.
clayis. See claith.
cled, clothed.
cleif, be split.
cleik, clutch.
clein(e), clene, quite, utterly.
cleir, clere, bright, beautiful.
cleith, clothe; clething, clothing.
clerk, cleric, scholar.
clever. See claver.
cleverus, nimble, adroit.
clewch, gorge, cliff; pl. clewis.
clift, fork of the thighs.
clip, call for, demand.
clips, clippis, eclipse.
clod, pelt.
clok, cloak.
clour, bump, swelling.
clowis, cluvis, claws.
clowttis, cloths, rags.
clud, cloud.
cluik, claw.
cluvis. See clowis.
clype, big softie.
coft, bought.
coillis, coals.
cok, cry, admit defeat.
cold, could, did.
collep, flagon.
colleveris, coal-horses.
commirwald, hen-pecked.

(142)

commissar, representative.

compeir, make a formal appearance, present.

compile, describe.

compt, account, reckon(ing).

concedring, considering.

conclusionis, inferences.

conditiounis, disposition.

confort, solace, please.

conjurit, charged.

considerance, reflection.

constance, steadfastness.

consuetude, custom, usage.

contenance, contynance, bearing, demeanour.

contenence, self-restraint.

continuatioun, succession.

continuit, adjourned.

contrariowsly, hostilely, perversely.

convenabille, fitting, appropriate.

convene, assemble.

convoy, (v.) convey, conduct; (n.) carriage.

cop, coup, cowp, cup. Play ∼ out, empty the bowl.

corpolent, large, bulky.

correnoch, coronach, outcry (Gaelic).

cors(e), (1) cross, (2) body, person.

cost, coast.

coud, cowd, cought, could, did.

count, female pudendum.

counyie, quicker of, quicker in coining (?); perh. as an alliterative tag, quicker.

courtly, elegant.

couth(e), cowth, cuth, could, knew how to.

cowhubye, booby, trifler.

cowit, cropped.

crab(b)it, crossed, ill-natured.

cradoun(e), crawdo(u)n, craven, coward.

craif, ask, demand.

craig, neck.

craikar, crakkar, boaster.

crak, noise.

crakkis, boasts, shouts.

cramase, crimson (cloth).

cran, cren, crane.

crap, crept.

crauch, cry, admit defeat.

craw, crow.

creddens, trust, credit.

creill, wicker basket.

creische, grease, fat.

croce, crose, cross, market-cross.

crok, old ewe.

crop(pis), shoot(s); ∼ and rute, paragon.

croppit, trimmed.

cropyn, crept.

crowdie mowdie, gruel of milk and meal; a term of endearment.

croynd, bellowed.

crudis, curds.

cruke, deformity, limp; cruikit, cruke, crooked.

cry, proclaim, call loudly for.

cryar, shouter, 'rowdie'.

crynd, withered, wasted.

Crysthinmes, Christmas.

cummer, trouble; cummerid, harassed, destroyed.

cum(m)er, gossip, crony; ∼lik, intimately, sociably.

cummin, cum(m)yn(e), *p.p.* come.

cunnyng, skill, learning.

cuntre, country.

cunyie, coin; cunyeitt, coined.

cunyour, coiner.

curage, curege, spirit; purpose; desire, lust; vigour; valour.

curat, priest, one having the cure of souls.

curche, kerchief.

cure, charge, office, function.

curio(u)s(e), curyus, subtle, ingenious, intricate, dainty.

curldodie, ribwort plantain.

cursing, coursing.

cursour, courser.

cuschett, wood-pigeon.

cusing, cousin, kinsman.

cutis, ankles.

daill, (1) dale, (2) part; sexual intercourse.

dait, time, limit.

dandely, darling, pet.

dane, haughty.

dang. See ding.

danger(e), denger, dominion; reluctance, coyness; fractiousness.

dant, subdue.

dar, dare.

darth, dearth.

dautit, petted.

daw, (1) dawn; (2) slattern.

daynte, favour, affection; delight.

debait, (v.) contend, defend, protect; (n.) strife; at debaittis, at variance.

de(e), die; ded(e), deid, dead.

dede, deid, deithe, death.

defend, resist.

deflorde, disfigured, marred.

degest, calm, considered.

deill, (1) bit, part; (2) devil; ～ a bit, not a bit.

deir, precious, important.

deis, dais, platform.

deliverance, action, agility.

deliverly, quickly.

dennar, dinner.

denty, esteem.

depaynt, painted, vivid.

depurit, purified.

deray, disorder, disturbance.

dergy, deirgey, dirge, funeral service.

derne, hidden, secret, private.

dert, dart.

dery dan, a dance; copulation. Cf. dirrye dantoun.

descry(ve), discri(v)e, describe.

despyt, dispyt, (v.) despise; (n.) indignation, animosity.

dessaveabille, deceitful.

detressit, untressed, loose.

devit, deafened.

devoit, devout; adv. devotely.

devyce, at, to his liking, perfectly.

deyne, disdain.

dicht, arrayed, prepared; dealt with.

diedie, active in, given to.

ding, strike, dash, overcome; *pa.t.* dang ; *p.p.* dungin.

ding, worthy.

dirk, dark; dirkit, darkened.

dirkin, lie hid, lurk.

dirrye dantoun, a dance. Cf. dery dan.

dise(i)s, trouble.

dispensationis, exemptions from religious duties.

dispern, dispel, drive away.

dispitous, contemptuous.

disport, pleasure, delight.

dispulit, despoiled.

dispyt. See despyt.

dissaif, deceive; dissavand, deceitful.

dissever, separation.

dissym(b)lit, disguised, counterfeit.

dissymilance, dissimulation.

disteyne, stain.

divinour, diviner, sage.

doig, dog.

dok, arse.

done, (1) do, (2) caused to; (*auxiliary*) ～ devour, devoured, &c.

donk, moist(en), wet.

doun(e), down; descended.

dour(e), stubborn.

doverrit, sunk in sleep, stupefied.

dow, dove.

dowbart, blockhead.

dowsy, stupid, ass.

dowt, uncertainty; but ～, assuredly.

draf(f), malt refuse, hog's-wash, dregs.

draif, drove, passed. Cf. dryfe.

dram, (*adj.*) sorrowful; (*n.*) melancholy.

drawkit, drenched.

dre, drie, endure, suffer.

dred, feared.

dreid, (for) fear; but ～, ～less, certainly, doubtless.

dres(s), address, prepare, treat, turn, betake.

drouthe, dryness, thirst.

drublie, clouded, troubled.
drug, drag, tug.
drup, **drowp**, droop, decline.
dryfe (our), drive, pass.
dub, puddle, stagnant pool.
duddroun, sloven.
duik, **duke**, duck.
duill, **dule**, (*n.*) sorrow, distress;
(*adj.*) sober.
dulce, sweet.
dully, dreary.
dungin. See **ding**.
dures, violence, harm.
duris, doors.
dwamyng, swooning.
dyk, wall.
dynnit, made a noise.
dynt, blow.
dyntie, delicacy.
dyt, (*v.*) write; (*n.*) writing.

e, **ee**, eye; *pl.* **ene**, **eyn(e)**.
edder, **eddir**, adder.
effect, value, worth.
effeir, behaviour, mien.
effeiritly, in terror.
eff(e)ray, (*n.*) terror, alarm; (*v.*)
terrify.
efter, after(wards); ∼**hend**, be-
hind, afterwards.
eik, **eke**, also.
e(i)ld, age.
e(i)rd, **erd(e)**, (*v.*) bury; (*n.*) earth.
ell, measure (about 3 feet).
ellis, else.
elrich(e), frightful, hideous,
weird.
elyk, alike.
emerant, emerald.
empryce, sovereign.
enbrast, embraced.
enchessoun, reason, objection.
endite, **endyte**, (*v.*) write; (*n.*)
composition.
endlang, along.
ene, **eyn(e)**. See **e**.
enermit, in arms.
engyne, **ingyne**, ingenuity, cun-
ning.
enlumyne, illuminate.

erand, **eirand**, petition, prayer;
errand.
ernis, eagles.
ers, arse.
Ersch(e), Gaelic.
eschame, be ashamed.
eschew, (1) gain, accomplish; (2)
avoid, shun, escape.
estait, rank; *pl.* ranks, classes
(the lords spiritual, lords tem-
poral, burgh commissioners).
estymet, estimated.
everilk, each.
evill willie, malevolent.
except, make a legal objection.
exerce, exercise, practise.

fa, foe.
facit, done up.
faculte, art, profession.
fader, father, old fellow.
failye, fail, lack.
fain, **fane**, willing(ly), glad(ly).
fairheid, beauty.
fairly. See **ferly**.
fald, fold, field.
fallow, (*v.*) associate with (*refl.*)
(5. 138); (*n.*) fellow, equal, com-
rade.
falset, falsehood.
familiar, servant.
fand, found.
fang, (*v.*) get, take; (*n.*) booty.
fannoun, maniple.
fantasy, apparition, illusion.
far, at a distance; ∼ **furth**, to
this extent.
fare, (1) fair, market; (2) expres-
sion, demeanour.
farleis. See **ferly**.
fartingaillis, hooped petticoats.
fary, (1) faery, fairyland; (2) tu-
mult.
fas(s)o(u)n, fashion.
favour, kindness; appearance.
feblit, enfeebled.
fecht, fight; *pa.t.* **faucht**.
fedder, feather.
fed(d)rem(e), **fethreme**, covering
of feathers.

feid, feud, enmity.

feill, (1) (*v.*) feel; (*n.*) understanding, sense; (2) many.

feir, (1) fear, (2) array; **feirris,** gestures, ways. See **fere.**

fek, (1) force; (2) main part.

felye, fail.

fend(e), **feynd,** **f(i)eind,** fiend, devil.

fene, **feny(i)e,** **feynye,** feign.

fensum, nauseous.

fenyeour, pretender, sham.

fer, far.

fere, **feir,** **feyr,** mate, comrade; (in) **fere,** (in) company; **in ~ of weir,** in warlike array; **but ~,** without equal.

ferleit, wondered.

ferly, fairly, wonder, marvel (*pl.* **farleis**); **~ful,** wonderful.

fers(e), fierce.

fervent, ardent, raging.

fethreme. See **fed(d)rem(e).**

fetrit, fastened.

feulis, birds.

fewte, fealty.

fillok, wench, wanton.

firth(e), wooded country.

flag, slut, hussy.

flane, flayn, arrow.

flaw, defect (forgery in legal deeds).

fle, (1) fly, escape; (2) frighten, chase.

fleggar, flatterer.

fleich, cajole; *n.* **fleichour,** coaxer.

fleis, flies.

fleme, banish.

flet, inner part of a house.

flete, fleit, (1) (*v.*) flow; (*n.*) flood; (2) scared.

flewme, phlegm.

flicht, (*v.*) fluctuate; (*n.*) flight.

flingar, dancer.

flocht, flutter(ing); instability.

flouris (grene), the most flourishing time of life.

flud(e), flood.

flure, floor.

flureis, flourish.

flyrok, deformed fellow.

flyt(e), scold, contend; **flyt(t)ing,** quarrel.

fog, coarse grass, left in the field in winter.

foir, fore; **~stair,** outside stair.

fone, (*v.*) be foolish, dote; (*adj.*) foolish.

for, on behalf of, because of.

forcely, powerfully.

forder, further.

foregrantschir, great-grandfather.

forfairn, worn out, perished.

forg(e)it, moulded, made.

forlane, laid aside, useless.

forleit, abandon(ed).

forloir, perish; (*p.p.*) **forlore,** lost.

forloppin, fugitive.

forriddin, overworked.

forrow, to, before.

forse, on, perforce, necessarily.

forthwart, forward.

forvayit, went astray.

foryhet, forget; forgotten.

fouth, fullness, bulk.

fow, full.

fra, fro, from, when.

frackar, livelier.

frak, move swiftly.

frawart, froward.

fray, alarm.

fre, noble, glorious.

fredom(e), nobility, generosity, free disposition.

freik, freke, fellow, man.

freir, friar.

fremmit, fremyt, strange, wild, hostile.

frog, coat, mantle.

front, forehead, face.

fruct, fruit; benefit.

frustar, idle, ineffectual; **in ~,** in vain.

frustrat, balked.

fucksail, foresail; (*transf.*) skirt.

fudder, futher, cartload, great number.

fude, food.

fuk, copulate.

fule, full, fool.

fullelie, foully, vilely.

fulyeit, exhausted.

fundin, found.

fur(e), went.

furght, furth(e), forth, continuously, prominently; ~ bering, bearing.

furtheyet, poured forth.

fut(t), foot; futt syd, reaching to the feet.

futher. See fudder.

fycket, fidgeted.

fyle, fyll, defile.

fyne, end.

fyreflaucht, ~flawcht, lightning.

ga, go, walk; *pa.t.* gaid ; *p.p.* gane.

gadderar, gatherer, miser.

ga(i)ff. See gif(f).

gaist, ghost, shadow, spirit.

gait, way.

galland, gallant, fine fellow.

gallous, gallow, gallows.

gam(e), pleasure, sport.

gammald, gamount, caper, frolic.

gan(e), face. See also ga.

ganestude, opposed.

gang, (*v.*) go, (*n.*) walk, tread.

gangarall, toad.

gany(i)e, arrow, dart.

gar, ger, make, force.

gardevyance, travelling trunk.

garesoun, garisoun, company, troop.

gartane, garter.

garth(e), garden.

gat, got.

gaw, gall-bladder.

gawfe, guffaw.

gawsy, handsome, jolly fellow.

geangleir, jangler.

geir, arms, costume, goods.

gek, derisive gesture.

gend, simple, foolish.

generale, in, without specific reference.

genner, beget.

gent, graceful, lovely.

gentill, well-born, noble.

gentrise, rank, nobility, courtesy.

genyie, disposition.

ger. See gar.

gett, (*v.*) beget; (*n.*) offspring.

gif(f), gife, give; *pa.t.* ga(i)f(f) ; *p.p.* gevin. Godgif, would that.

gif(e), if. bot ~, unless.

gild, clamour, din.

gillet, mare.

gin, gyn, wile, contrivance; siege-engine.

girn, gyrn, grimace, snarl.

girnall, granary.

girt. See gre(i)t.

girth, safety, sanctuary, refuge.

gladderit, besmeared.

gla(i)d, (*adj.*) glad, (*v.*) rejoice, applaud; gladar, gledar, one who makes glad.

glaikis, deception, folly, sexual desire.

glar, mud.

gle, melody, mirth; ~man, minstrel.

gled, kite.

gledar. See glaid.

glengoir, pox(ed).

glete, glitter, gleam.

gleyd, ember.

glour, glowr, stare, scowl.

glyd(e), move, flow.

go, walk; go or ryde, go; gois behynd, takes second place.

goif, gaze; *pa.t.* govit.

golk, cuckoo.

goreis, filth (? rheum).

gorgeit, stopped up.

gormaw, cormorant.

gossip, companion, fellow.

goulis, heraldic red.

goun, gown.

govirnance, rule, conduct.

govit. See goif.

gowdye, ? goldy, goldfinch.

graceles, ill-favoured, ugly.

graip, handle, feel.

graith, make ready; *pa.t.* grathit.

grane, groan.

grantschir, grandfather.

grayne, branch.

gre, prize.
greceles, ill-favoured fellow.
gree, agree.
greif, offend, afflict.
gre(i)t, grete, weep.
gre(i)t, grit, gryt(t), girt, great.
grephoun, griffin.
gress, gris, grass.
grippis, grasp, embrace.
grit, gyrt. See gre(i)t.
groukar, (obscure).
grundyn, ground, sharpened.
gruntill, gruny(i)e, snout.
gryce, sucking pig.
guberne, govern.
gud(e), guid, good; gudame, grandmother.
gukit, guckit, daft; gukkis, ? fool (term of endearment).
gutar, gutter.
gyand, gyane, giant.
gymp, graceful, slender.
gyng, company.
gys(e), gy(i)s, way, style, attire; masquerade, entertainment.

haggeis, haggis.
haif(f), have.
haiknay, horse.
haill, hale, whole, wholly; ~sum, wholesome, sweet.
hair(e), hoary.
hairt, hart(e), hert, heart; ~fully, heartily; ~ly, affectionate.
hait, hett, hot.
hald, hold, consider, keep; p.p. haldin.
halflingis, half, partly.
hals, neck, throat.
halse, greet, salute; pa.t. halsit, embraced.
haly, holy.
hame, home.
hang, hung.
hankersaidil, anchorite.
hant, resort, company.
happit, covered.
hard(e), heard.
hardy, bold; ~ment, boldness.
harlett, harlott, rascal; whore.

harlit, dragged.
harnas, harnes, equipment, armour.
harnis, brains.
harth, hard.
hat, pa.t. hit.
hatrent, hatred.
hautand, hawtane, proud.
havie, havy, heavy; ~nes, despair.
having, demeanour.
haw, livid.
hawkit, white-streaked (of cattle).
he, heich, hie, high; ~nes, highness, majesty.
hecht, named, promised.
hed. See hef(f).
hef(f), have; pa.t. hed.
heft, haft.
hegeit, hedged, bordered.
heggirbald, (?); -bald is a pejorative suffix in Dunbar.
heich. See he.
heid, head.
heildit, helit, covered, concealed.
heilie, haughty.
heilis, heylis, heels.
heill, health.
heklis, scratches.
hel(l)and, heleand, highland.
helit. See heildit.
helpis (fra), relieves (from).
hend(e), heynd, skilled; courteous, gentle; pleasant.
herbrit, harboured.
herreit, heryit, harried, robbed.
hes, has, have.
hett. See hait.
hew, hue; hewit, coloured.
heynd. See hend(e).
hicht, height.
hiddous, hiddowis, hoddous, hideous.
hiddy giddy, topsy-turvy; in a whirl.
hing, hyng, hang.
hint, (n.) grip, clutch; (v.) caught; hynting, grasp.
hir, her.
hirklis, contract, crouch.
hirpland, limping.

his, its.
hobbell clowttar, cobbler.
hobbillschowe, commotion.
hobland, hobbling.
hoddous. See hiddous.
hodiern, of today, now.
hog, young sheep.
hogeart, ? jogger, fidgeter.
hoip, houp, howp, hope.
holkit, hollow.
holyn, holly.
homecyd, (n.) manslayer; (adj.)
    murderous.
hommiltye jommeltye, ? clumsy.
hopschackellt, secured by a hob-
hospitall, lodging.   [ble.
host, cough.
houris, hours; prayers at stated
    times.
hous, hows, house; horsecloth.
howffing, clumsy fellow.
howlat, howle, owl.
hud pyk, miser.
hudit, hooded.
hukebane, haunch bone.
hunder, hundreth, hundred.
hungert, starved.
hurcheo(u)n(e), hedgehog.
hurdar, hoarder.
hurle bawsy, ? term of endear-
    ment. Hurlbasie is the name of
    a spirit in *The Freiris of Berwik*.
hyd, hide, skin.
hyndir, last.
hyne, hence.

ilk, same, each; ilka, each.
illustare, illustrious.
imprent, impress on the mind.
impyre, rule.
inclyne, bow (towards).
indeficient, unfailing.
indoce, endorse; indo(i)st, en-
    dorsed.
indyt(t), write, compose.
infe(c)k, (be) infect(ed); ~fra, in-
    capable of.
inferne, infernal; below.
ingynour, contriver.
innis, lodging, house.

inthrang, shoved in.
in to, intill, into, in, at, on.
ische, issue.
iwis(e), certainly.

ja, jay.
jakkis, quilted coats, leather or
    plated; ? knaves, 30. 39.
jevellour, jailer.
jolie, joly, lively; pretty, splen-
    did; arrogant, overbearing.
Jow, Jew, heathen.
joy, enjoy.
juffler, ? shuffler, bungler.
jurdane, chamber-pot.
jure, law.

kay, jackdaw.
keik, peep.
keist, kest, cast.
kell, head-dress.
kem, comb.
kempe, champion.
ken, know.
kene, keyne, bold, fierce.
kep, catch.
kers, cress, something worthless.
kethat, garment.
kinrik, kingdom.
kirsp, a delicate fabric.
kist, chest, box.
kith, country.
knaw, (1) know, (2) gnaw.
kneff, servant.
knitchell, small bundle.
knop, bud.
knowll tais, knobbed toes.
knyp, nibble.
kokenis, ? rogues.
koy, quey, heifer.
kyn, race.
kynd, (n.) nature, race; (adj.)
    generous, well-bred; ~nes,
    nature; love.
kyth, show, discover.

lachtter. See lawchtir.
laeffe, laif, rest, remainder.
laid, fellow.
la(i)k, (1) lack; (2) fight.
lake, (running) water.

laip, lap.
lair(e), learning, instruction.
laiseir, leisure.
laith, (n.) harm; (adj.) unwilling;
~ly, loathsome.
lait(t)is, manners, disposition.
lame, lameness.
landit, possessed of land.
lang(e), long; ~syne, long ago.
lanis, conceals.
lap, leapt.
lape, tucked up.
larbar, impotent (fellow).
larges, generosity.
lassis, (inexperienced) girls.
lat(t), prevent. See also leit.
lauch, laugh; pa.t. lewch(e),
luche.
laureat(e), distinguished; emi-
nent in poetry.
law, low.
lawchtir, lachtter, laughing (mat-
ter).
lawd, (1) loud; (2) common, vulgar.
le(y), lie.
leche, le(i)ch(e), physician.
le(i)d, (1) person, man; (2) lan-
guage; (3) lead (metal).
ledder, (1) leather, (2) ladder.
legeand, history, account.
leich, leash.
leif, lef(e), leve, (1) leave, (2)
live, (3) leaf (pl. leiffis, lev(e)is).
leifis me, is dear to me.
le(i)ge, subject.
leill, lele, true, loyal.
leir, leyr, learn.
leit, lete, lett, lat, allow, let.
leme, gleam; lemys, rays.
Lentern, Lentrune, Lent.
lern, teach.
les of, lessen.
lesing, lie.
lest, last, least.
leuket, looked.
leve. See leif.
levefull, lawful.
levir, rather.
lewch(e). See lauch.
licht, lycht, (1) light, (2) alight.

lif, lyf(f), lyve, (v.) live; (n.) life;
~ly, lively; on ~, alive.
lift, sky.
lig, lie.
linege, linnage, family, race.
lippir, leper.
lisk, flank.
list, wish.
listly, craftily, easily.
loffit, lovit, praised.
loik, luke-, warm-(hearted).
loikman, hangman.
lonye, lunyie, loin.
losinger, deceiver.
louket, looked.
loun, lown, fellow, rogue.
loungeour, lounger, good-for-
nothing.
lour, scowl.
lous, lows, loose.
lout(t), lowt, bow down.
lovery, (livery), allowance.
loving, praise.
lovit. See loffit.
low, flame.
lucerne, lamp.
luche. See lauch.
lude, love, be fond of (drink).
luf(f), lufe, luif, love; luffer,
luifar, lover.
lufraye, livery, costume.
lug, ear.
luge(ing), lodging, dwelling.
lu(i)k(e), look.
lunyie. See lonye.
lurdane, idler.
lust, joy, desire.
lustie, lusty, joyful, lively, gaily
dressed; vigorous (person).
lyart, gray.
lychtleit, despised.
lyk, like; as it was ~, as it chose;
lykand, pleasing.
lymmar, knave; adj. ~(full).
lynd, tree.
lyne, lain.
lyntall, lintel.
lyre, flesh.
lys, lice.
lyth(is), (imp.) listen.

lyve. See lif.

ma, ma(i)r, mare, more.
ma(c)kar, maker, poet.
macull, stain.
magnificence, bounty, glory.
magryme, migraine.
maid, maed, made; *p.p.* written verses.
maik, mate; ∼les, matchless.
ma(i)r. See ma.
maist, maest, most.
maister, master; Master of Arts.
mak, (*v.*) make, compose, (*n.*) nature, sort.
makdome, comeliness.
man, mon, must.
mank, flaw.
mannace, menace, threat(en); *n.* manas(s)ing.
mansuetude, mildness, gentleness.
markis, signs; seal.
marleyon, merlin.
marrit, frightened.
Martis, (of) Mars.
mastevlyk, like a mastiff.
matern, maternal.
matutyne, morning.
mauch, ? thief.
mavessie, malmsey (sweet wine).
mavis, mavys, thrush.
maw, sea-gull.
may, can, has power (to).
mayit, celebrated May, made merry.
med, set.
me(i)kill, me(i)kle, much, great.
mein, menis, means.
meir, mare.
mell, meddle; mix, copulate.
mellie, skirmish, combat.
mene, complain. See also mein.
menstrallie, minstrelsy.
mensweir, forswear.
menyie, (1) company, following, (2) stain, (3) pain, hurt.
menys, take pity on.
merk, approach.
merk, mirk, dark(ness).
merle, blackbird.

merrens, ? wretchedness.
mes, mass.
messan, lap-dog.
methis (? *for* nechis), draws (near).
micht, mycht, might; *adv.* mychttelye.
midding, midden.
migarnes, leanness.
mirry, merry; *comp.* mirrear.
mischief, harm, misfortune.
mismak, make wrongly.
mittan, myttane, hawk.
modern, existing now.
moir, more.
mokis, mak, deride.
mon. See man.
mone, moyne, moon.
moneth, month.
monsour, gentleman.
morgeownis, grimaces, antics.
morow(ing), morning.
morthour, murder.
most, must.
mot, may.
mowaris, mockers (at the moon), foolish idlers.
mowlis, chilblains.
muddir, muder, mother.
munyoun, darling.
myance, resource.
mychane, (*obscure*).
mychar, pilferer, sneak-thief.
mylne, mill.
mynnye, mother.
mynting, attempt.
mys, sin.

na, no; nor, than.
nackettis, ball-boys.
naem, name.
nagus, miser.
nain, nane, none.
nanis, for the, on purpose, for the occasion.
nar, neir, near.
ne(i)d, need; of necessity; it nedis, it is necessary (for).
neir, (1) near(ly), almost, (2) never.
neis, nose.

nipcaik, miser, cheese-parer.
nocht, noucht, not; nothing.
noddill, head.
nolt, cattle.
nor, than.
note, make use of.
nothair, nowdir, nowthir, neither.
noy, annoyance, distress.
nuke, corner.
nureis, nurse.
nurtir, nurtour, breeding, discipline.
nyce, nyse, foolish; strange; wanton, flamboyant.
nychtbour, neighbour.
nyghttit, benighted.

observance, ceremony, worship, ordinance.
ocht, aught, anything.
ockerar, usurer.
one, on; on(e) to, ontill, unto, to.
onis, once.
onone, anon, at once.
onrycht, wrongly.
ontill. See one.
ony, any.
oppin, open.
or, ere; if not.
oratrice, (fem.) petitioner.
ordynance, instruments of war.
ornat, embellished, eloquent.
ost, host.
ostir, oyster.
ouer, ou(i)r, ower, over; too.
ouerse, overlook.
ouirgane, overcome, taken.
ourgilt, gilded over.
ourscailit, dappled, flecked.
ourstred, bestrode.
ourtane, overtaken.
ourthort, across.
owdir, owther, either.
owk, week.
owsprang, sprang out.
oxstar, armpit.

pacok, pako, peacock.
padgeane, padyane, pageant, entertainment.

page, fellow, member of the lower orders.
paikis, blows, punishment.
paill, pall, canopy.
pairt(e), (n.) part; (v.) depart.
paitlat, neckerchief, collar, ruff.
palestrall, palatial.
pallatt, head.
pane, pain, misery.
panence, penance, penitence.
pansches, tripe.
panton, slipper.
papingo, parrot; pl. papingais.
parage, rank.
parde, indeed, verily.
parroche, parish.
Pasche, Pesche, Easter.
pastance, pastime, pleasure.
pavys, large shield; protection.
peax, peace.
pechis, panting, laboured breathing.
pedder, pedlar.
peilit, peld, plucked bare.
peir, equal.
peirt, pert, sprightly, brisk; comp. adv. pertlyar.
pelo(u)r, thief.
pen(n)is, feathers, quills.
persew, pursue, frequent.
pert, brisk, lively.
pertrik, partridge.
perverst, perverted.
pete, pety, p(i)etie, pity. See 10. 49, note.
peur, pur(e), poor.
phisnomy, face.
pillie, ? colt (? F. poulain).
pin, gallows.
piscence, power.
pische, piss, urinate.
pladdis, plaids of woollen (tartan) cloth.
plane, sheer, manifest; flat, naked; in ~, plainly, directly.
plane, pleyne, pleinyie, complain.
pleis, (v.) please; (n.) pleasure: plesance, plesans, plesere, delight.

plet, intertwined.
plever, plover.
pley, merriment.
pleyne. See **plane.**
plicht anker, main anchor.
pluch, plough.
plukkis, steals.
plum, round, well-filled.
plunge, pool.
ply, condition.
polesie, improvement, embellishment (of a town, building).
polk, sacking; bag.
polt, bang, knock.
port, (1) gate, (2) carriage, manner.
portratour, portrature, appearance, form.
possest, established.
possodie, sheep's head broth.
pot, pit, abyss.
potestatis, powers, rulers.
potingar, apothecary.
pottingry, pharmacy.
pow, pull.
practik, practice.
prattelie, prettily.
preclair, famous.
pre(i)che, preach; **pre(i)ching**, religious service.
preif(f), preve, proof, prove.
preis, pres, (v.) press, go, strive; (n.) crowd, conflict.
prel(l)at, prelot, prelate; priest.
prent, impression.
presandlie, presently.
preve(ly), secret(ly).
prevene, get before, forestall.
preving, proving.
pricklous, tailor (derisive).
prik, skewer.
probatioun, demonstration.
proces, argument, delay.
proclame, denounce.
proffeit, common, general good; ∼, **singular**, personal advantage.
promyt, promise.
propyne, present, give.
pryce, prys, value.
pulder, powder.

pultre, chickens.
pur(e). See **peur.**
purgation, purgative.
purpest, purposed.
purp(o)ur, purpyr, purple.
pusoun, poison.
pychar, pitcher.
pyk, thorn.
pyne, pain, anguish.
pynit, shrivelled, withered.
pyot, magpie.

quair, book.
quell, kill, destroy, knock down.
quene, quein, (1) queen, (2) hussy, strumpet.
quer(r)ell, cause; complaint, altercation.
quha(i), who; **quhais, quhois(e)**, whose; **quham, quhom(e)**, whom; **quhasa**, whoever.
quha(i)l, whale.
quha(i)r, where.
quhat-throu, because of.
quheil(l), wheel.
quhen, quhone, when.
quhene, few.
quhilis, quhilum, at times.
quhilk, which.
quhill, while, till.
quhillelillie, penis.
quhit, quhyt(e), quhytt, white, specious.
quhone. See **quhen.**
quhorle, whirl.
quhou, quhow, how.
quhryne, squeal.
quintiscence, quintessance, the 'fifth essence', of which the heavenly bodies were thought to be composed, and the extraction of which was one of the objects of alchemy.
quitt, repay.
quyk, quik, alive, vital; **quykkin**, vitalize.
quyte, quite; quit. mak ∼, make a clearance.

radius, radyous, radiant.

raid, rode.

raif, (1) rave, talk passionately, (2) tore.

raip, rope.

rair, roar; scream.

rais(e), raise; *pa.t.* rose.

rak, crack; quhatt ∼, what matter. See rakles.

rak sauch, gallows-bird.

rakit, went.

rakkettis, tennis rackets.

rakles, heedless, rash.

raly(i)e, jest.

rame, scream, cry.

ranso(u)n, raunson, ransom.

rap, strike, dash.

rasoun, reason.

ravyne, voracity; fowll of ∼, bird of prey.

raw, row.

rawcht, reached.

rawchtir, rafter, rough beam.

rax, stretch.

rebald, worthless, base; scurrilous.

reboytit, repulsed.

rebuik, reproach, reproof.

rebute, repulse.

reche, rich, fine.

recryat, recant.

red(d)our, fear.

re(i)d(e), (*v.*) read, advise; (*adj.*) red; (*pp.*) frightened; (*n.*) fear.

reffus, renounce.

reflex, reflection.

refute, defence, protection; stronghold.

regratour, retailer.

regyne, queen.

rehator, enemy.

reik, reke, smoke.

rejosing, source of gladness.

relation, narrative, account.

relevis, supports, helps.

religious, belonging to a religious order.

remeid, remedy, help.

remuffit, removed, lifted.

renyie, reynye, rein. See also 30. 78, note.

repair, resort, haunt, usual abode.

repreif(f), reprove.

requeir, ask.

re(i)rd, noise, tumult.

rere, roar.

ressaif, ressave, receive.

rethor, rhetorician, master of eloquence; rethorie, rhetoric.

retreitit, reversed.

r(e)uth, rewth, compassion, pity.

revar, robber, raider.

revest, clothed.

revin, raven. See also ryf(f).

rew, (1) regret, (2) the herb rue.

riall, ryall(e), ryell, royal, noble, splendid.

riatus, boisterous.

rift, belch.

rigbane, backbone.

rilling, shoe made of undressed hide.

ring, reign; *pa.t.* rong.

rise, ryce, branch, brushwood.

risp, sedge.

roch, rock.

rocht, wrought.

rolp, rowp, shout hoarsely, bawl.

rong. See ring.

ronk, luxuriant, dense.

ros, rois, rosyne, rose; rosere, rose-bush.

roun(e), rown, whisper; done ∼, talked with; rownar, tattler.

roust, rust.

routt, rowt, company.

rowp. See rolp.

rowt, (1) blow; (2) scour.

roy, king.

rubeatour, rogue.

ruch, rough.

rude, (1) cross, (2) rough.

rug, tug, draw.

ruge, roar.

rumpill, fold; rumple, tail.

runsy, rouncy, horse.

rycht, right.

ryf(f), ryfe, tear, split, crack; *p.p.* revin.

ryn, run.

ryne, rind, bark.

rys(e), rise.

sa, so, on condition that.

sacrand, sacring; sacring bell, bell rung at the consecration of the Host.

saek, saik, sake.

saep, soap.

saikles, innocent.

saily(i)e, attack.

sair, sar, sore, sorely; *comp.* sarar.

sait(t), seat, court.

sall, shall; salbe, shall, shalt, be.

salt, assault.

salue, salus(e), greet, make salutation.

salvatour, saviour; (*fem.*) salvatrice.

sam, samin, samyn(e), same.

sanative, healthful.

sanct, saint.

sane, bless; sanyne, blessing.

sang, song.

sark, serk, shirt.

sary, sorry, wretched.

saul(e), saull, sawle, soul.

saw, speech, utterance, discourse.

sax, six.

sayn, sene, say, tell.

scaffar, sponger.

scail, scale, disperse, spill; *pa.t.* skaild.

scamler, parasite.

scart, scratch.

scattis, skates.

schaiffyne, shaved.

schalk, man, fellow.

schau, saw.

schaw(e), (*v.*) show, (*n.*) thicket, wood.

sche, scho(u), she.

sched, part, divide.

schell, (shell-shaped) vulva.

schend, schent, confound.

schene, bright.

schepe, plan, set oneself; *pa.t.* schup(e).

scherp, (*adj.*) sharp, (*v.*) sharpen.

schevill, distorted, twisted.

schew, showed.

schewre, tore off.

schill, shrill.

schilling, husks.

schir, sir.

scho(u). See sche.

schog, shake, rock.

schoir, schore, (*v.*) threaten, (*n.*) threat, menace.

schomd, ? adorned.

schone, shoes.

schort, (*adj.*) short, (*v.*) shorten.

schot, shooting.

schoud, (*obscure*).

schour, shower.

schow, shove; n. schowar.

schrenk, shrink.

schrew, (*v.*) beshrew, curse, (*n.*) villain, devil.

schrift, confession, revelation.

schroud, covered.

schrowd, garment, clothing.

schulder, shoulder; schulderar, shover.

schup(e). See schepe.

schyre, bright, clear.

sciens, knowledge.

scopin, half-pint.

scull, school.

scunner, disgust.

scutarde, evacuator, skitterer.

se, see; *p.p.* se(i)ne, seyne.

sege, (1) man, (2) siege.

seik(nes), sick(ness).

seir, many.

sek, sack.

sekerly. See sicir.

sell, self.

sell, to, for sale.

sely, simple, good.

seme, appear (to be present).

sempitern, everlasting.

sen, since; ~syne, since then.

sence, incense.

sene. See sayn; se.

sentence, matter, thought.

senyie, (1) war-cry; (2) company.

serk. See sark.

sers, search.

sett by, accounted as worth.
sew, sue, woo.
sic, siclyke, sik, such. See be.
sich, sigh.
sicht, sight.
sicir, sicker, sure, safe; *adv.* sekerly.
sile, mislead (cover the eyes).
sircumstance, elaborate detail.
sittin, seated.
skaff, beg meanly.
skaild. See scail.
skaith, harm.
skar, scar, frighten; take fright.
skarth, monster.
skeil, pail.
skellat, small bell.
skill, basket.
skolder, scorch.
skrip, mock.
skrumple, wrinkle.
skryke, screech.
skrymming, darting.
skyis, clouds.
skynk, serve, pass.
skyre, ? scratch.
sla, kill, destroy.
slawchtir, slaughter.
slawsy, ? term of endearment.
slewth, sluggishness, tardiness.
slie, sle, wily, subtle.
slokyn, quench, sate.
slomer, slummer, slumber.
sloppis, bands.
slute, sluttery, slovenly.
slyding, slippery, unstable.
small, slender, weak; light (ale).
smorit, smothered.
smowk, smuke, smoke.
smydy, smithy, forge.
sobir(ly), quiet(ly), (decorously).
socht, sought, searched; fell.
soft, soften; ～ and fair, gently.
soin, son(e), soon, forthwith.
soir, sore(ly).
soldan(e), sowdan, sultan, ruler; ～land, Egypt (or adjacent lands).
song, sang.
sort, company.

sossery, sorcery.
souk, sowk, suck; soukar, sucker, sponger; sowklar, suckling.
soun(e), sowne, (1) sound, (2) son.
sounyie, care.
soup, sowp, sup.
southin, southerly.
soutter, sowter, cobbler.
soverane, supreme, excellent.
sowch, sighing.
sowld. See suld.
spald, limb.
spane, wean.
sparhalk, sparrow-hawk.
speciall, in, specifically.
speid, (*v.*) prosper, hasten, succeed; good～, quickly.
speir, (1) spear, (2) sphere, (3) ask.
spirling, smelt.
splene, heart.
spreit, spirit, ghost.
sprent, sprang.
spring, contest.
spruning, sticking out.
spryng, dancing tune.
spynist, opened out, blown.
squische, crop, crunch.
stacker, stagger.
staigis, steps.
stalit, urinated.
stalkar, poacher.
stall, stole, crept.
stanchell, kestrel.
stane, stone.
stang, sting; pole; penis.
stanneris, river gravel.
stark, stern, fierce; rigid, stiff.
starvit, perished.
statur, state, condition.
staw, stall.
stayd, steid, stead, place.
steill, (steel) armour.
steir, (*v.*) move, steer; (*n.*) on ～, astir, in a state of commotion.
stent, stretch.
ster, stern(e), star.
stern, resolute.
stevin, noise, sound, voice.

stirk, young bullock.

stok, trunk, stump.

sto(m)mok, stomach; stomacher, waistcoat.

storkyn, stiffen.

stound, sudden pain.

stour(e), conflict.

stowin, stolen.

stowp, tankard.

stra(e), straw.

stra(i)k, (*v. pa.t.*) struck; (*n.*) stroke, blow.

strait, stretch.

stramp, trample.

strand, stream.

strang, strong.

strange, strenge, distant, unfriendly, unfamiliar, unnatural.

straucht, straight.

strene, bind, draw tight.

strenewite, vigorousness.

strenge. See **strange.**

strummall, strumill, staggering, stumbling.

stryd, bestride, straddle.

strynd, race, lineage.

stryppis, armour.

stude, stood.

study, anvil.

sturt, discord, vexation; violence.

stychling, rustling.

style, (*v.*) give a title, (*n.*) name.

styng, pole.

stynt, stop.

sua, swa, so.

substantious, weighty, effective.

sueir, sweir, lazy, reluctant; ∼**nes,** sloth.

sueit, suete, sweet.

sueving, swevyng, dream.

suld, sould, sowld, should, might, had to, would, could.

sum, some, one (man).

sunye, hesitate.

super, over; ∼**expendit,** bankrupt.

superne, on high, dwelling in heaven.

supple, help, deliver (from).

suppos, although.

suppryis, (*v.*) do violence, harm, (*n.*) violence.

surmunting, surpassing.

surrigianis, surgeons.

sustene, endure, be equal to.

suth, (*n.*) truth; (*adj.*) true.

swaittis, small beer.

swak, hard blow.

swalme, swelling.

swanking, swanky, fine fellow.

swappit, ? big.

sweir, swear. See also **sueir.**

sweit, sweat.

swentyour, rascal.

swe(y)rd, sword.

swirk, spring forth.

swyr, hollow.

swyth, quickly.

syd, long; **on** ∼, askance.

syn, sin.

syn(e), then.

sys(e), times; **of sys,** often.

ta, tane, the one; **the tane,** that one.

taikinis, tokens, signs.

tail(l), (1) tale; (2) tail, train.

tailyour, telyour, tailor.

taingis, tongs.

tait, active, nimble.

tak, take; *p.p.* **tane, tein; takkar,** thief.

tald, tauld, tawld, told.

tane. See **ta; tak.**

targe, light shield.

tarmegant, boisterous, savage fellow.

tarsall, peregrine falcon.

tauch, tallow.

tedder, tether, gallows-rope.

tein. See **tak; tene.**

teme, tume, empty; *pa.t.* **temit, tomit.**

tending, moving; **tendit,** moved.

tene, te(i)n(e), teyne, (*v.*) vex; (*n.*) anger, vexation.

terand, ruffian, villain.

tern(e), (n.) vicissitude; (adj.) fierce.

terse, penis.

test, (1) taste; (2) trial.

tha(i), thay, they, those; tha(i)m, thame, them; thair, their.

tha(i)r-, there-; ~furth, forth from there.

than(e), then.

thar, there.

that, (so) that; what.

the, the; thee; these.

theis, thighs.

theolog(g)is, theologians.

thesaurer, treasurer.

think, it seems; pa.t. tho(u)cht.

thir, ther, these.

thirsill, thistle.

this, thus.

thocht, thoght, (n.) thought, care, perplexity, (v.) pa.t. reminded; ~ lang, yearned.

thocht, tho(u)ght, although.

thoill, thole, endure, suffer.

thrang, throng.

thraw, turn.

threpe, affirm, assert.

thrift, prosperity.

thrimlar, jostler.

thrist, (n.) thirst, (v.) thrust; thristar, shover.

thropill, thrapple, throat.

throu, throw, thr(o)uch(t), through.

thrungin, pressed, crushed.

thyne, thence.

till, to.

tinsale, loss.

tint. See ty(i)ne.

tirvit, stripped.

tod, fox.

tomit. See teme.

tone, tune.

to-schuke, shook violently.

tour, tower.

towdie, female pudendum.

towk, took.

townage, townysche, uncourtly.

tragidie, tragic narrative in verse.

tram, shaft.

tramort, corpse.

trapperis, trappouris, trappings.

trappit, adorned.

tra(y)ne, snare, treachery, guile.

treis, trees, bushes; sticks.

tre(i)t, entertain; tretable, tractable.

trest, trust.

trone, throne; tron.

trulis, ? bowls.

trumpour, impostor, trifler.

tryackill, medicine for venomous bites and malignant diseases.

trymbill, trymmill, tremble; pa.t. trymlit.

tryumph, achievement; glory.

tua, tuo, twa(y), two.

tuichandly, violently, persistently.

tuik, tuk(e), took.

tume. See teme.

turkas, blacksmith's pincers.

turse, truss, carry.

turto(u)r, turtle-dove.

tute mowitt, with a protruding mouth.

tuyse, twice.

tyde, water.

tydis, befalls.

ty(i)ne, lose; p.t. tint, tynt.

tyrlie myrlie, ? term of endearment.

tyt(e), quickly.

tythingis, news.

ud(d)er, udir, uthair, uthir, (each) other.

uly, oil.

unabaisitly, (adv.) unabashed.

uncow, uncouth, unknown, strange.

uncunnandly, unwittingly.

unfulyeit, unspoiled.

unneis, hardly, scarcely.

unsall, unhallowed.

unsleipit, not having slept.

unspaynit, unweaned.

unto, to, as far as, even to, in the state of.

upaland, in the country; upo-
    landis, countrified.
upheyt, exalted.
upskail, scatter, raise.

vane organis, veins.
vant, boasting.
vapour, mist.
vardour, verdure.
variand, various; varians, change.
vassalage, knightly prowess.
vawart, vanguard.
velves, velvot, velvet.
vennaum, venom; virulent lan-
    guage.
vertew, beneficial properties.
victrice, (fem.) conqueror.
voce, voice.
vode, destitute.
vostour, braggart.
vyce, wicked thing.

waes me, woe is me.
waett, wait, know(s); pa.t. wist.
waill, wale, choose.
waire, sea-weed (fig.).
waistie, desolate.
waistles, fat.
wait, (1) watch, wait; (2) wet.
    See also waett.
waithman, wathman, hunter,
    outlaw.
wald, would.
walk(in), waken; pa.t. waiknit,
    walknit, wouk(e).
wall, well, source.
wallidrag, weakling.
wallie, handsome, fine.
wallow, roll, flounder.
wam(b)e, belly; womb.
wan. See win.
wand, slender pliant stick.
wane, dwelling.
want, lose.
wantoun, sportive, reckless.
war, (1)were; (2)worse; (3)aware.
waris out, expend.
wark, werk, wirk, work.
warld, great quantity; war(l)dly,
    worldly, temporal.

warlo, scoundrel, devil.
warly, warlike.
warsill, wrestle; cf. werslingis.
wattis, welts.
waucht, quaff.
wawis, walls.
weche, watchman.
wed, mortgage.
we(i)d, dress.
we(i)do, wedow, widow.
weill, wel(l). ~ is me, happy am
    I; ~fair, happiness.
weir, wear.
weir, were, war.
weir, doubt, distress; but ~,
    withowttin ~, doubtless,
    indeed.
weld, command, possess.
wend, wene, think; pa.t. wend,
wer, wire.   [wen(i)t.
werblis, warbling.
werslingis, wrestling matches.
westar, waster.
wichis, witches.
wicht, weycht, wycht, fellow.
wicht, wight, wycht, strong;
    ~nes, strength.
wickir, branch.
widdy, withy, gallows-rope.
wif, woman.
wilk, whelk.
win, gain, achieve, triumph; pa.t.
    wan; wynning, profit.
windir, wondir, wonder(ful); (adv.)
    remarkably.
wirk furthe, work out, exhaust.
wirry, worry.
wirschip, honour.
wis, wyce, wys, wise, clever.
wist. See waett.
wit, understanding, discretion;
    ~ ye, (v.) you may be sure.
with, by, with.
wlonk, splendid, gorgeous (wo-
    man).
wod, woid, mad, fierce; ~nes,
    fierceness.
woddis, woods.
woddit, married.
wolroun, boar (abusive).

womple, wimple.

woord, wourd, word.

wosp, bundle of straw (as an ale-house sign).

wouk(e). See walk(in).

wow, woo.

wox, waxed.

wrait, wrayt, wret, wrote.

wreik, avenge.

wretche, wreche, villain, miser.

wrettingis, directions.

wrink, trick.

wrocht, wrought, caused.

wryng, wring the hands.

wy, (1) man, (2) way, manner.

wyld, combed.

wyppit, tied.

wyrok, corn.

wyt, blame.

ya, ye, yes.

yaid, yald, worn-out horse.

yadswyvar, one who practises bestiality.

yak, ache.

yarrow, the herb milfoil.

yawmer, yell, querulous cry.

yeid, went.

yemit, kept.

yerne, desire.

yet(t), gate.

yfere, in company, together.

ying, yong, young.

yoldyn, yielded.

yone, yonder.

Youll, Yu(i)ll, Yule.

yowle, yell.

yrne, iron.

PRINTED IN GREAT BRITAIN
AT THE UNIVERSITY PRESS, OXFORD
BY VIVIAN RIDLER
PRINTER TO THE UNIVERSITY